*Heinemann Organization
in Schools Series*

Head of Department

Head of Department:

*leading a department
in a comprehensive school*

Michael Marland

Headmaster
Woodberry Down School
London

Heinemann Educational Books
London

Heinemann Educational Books Ltd
LONDON EDINBURGH MELBOURNE AUCKLAND TORONTO
HONG KONG SINGAPORE KUALA LUMPUR NEW DELHI
NAIROBI JOHANNESBURG LUSAKA IBADAN
KINGSTON

ISBN 0 435 80585 1
Paperback ISBN 0 435 80576 2

Published by Heinemann Educational Books Ltd
48 Charles Street, London W1X 8AH
Printed Offset Litho and bound in Great Britain by
Cox & Wyman Ltd, London, Fakenham and Reading

CONTENTS

for my parents

Acknowledgements

My major debt is obvious, and I am very pleased to be able to record it in print: to the members of the two English Departments of which I was head: at Abbey Wood School, S.E.2, and Crown Woods School, S.E.9. I am grateful for all that I have learnt from them, and the pleasure and stimulation of working with such colleagues. I should like to thank specifically one: Marilyn Davies, who for over six years was an outstanding Deputy Head and then Head of Department at Crown Woods School, and whose understanding of the needs of a large department and ability to translate it into effective action are exceptional. I should also like to thank Gwen Evans, who read a draft of the first half of the book, and made a number of helpful suggestions.

I have been unusually lucky in having worked as Head of Department under two Head Teachers whose encouragement and understanding were exceptional: Mrs Y. B. Zackerwych and M. K. Ross. My debt to them goes far beyond the contents of this book.

I must, however, make it quite clear that this book is not written solely out of my personal experience, but it has been extensively supplemented by observation of other schools and discussion with teachers working elsewhere. Thus, the good ideas and procedures described have not necessarily been put into practice by me, nor are the bad examples included for comparison necessarily drawn from the schools in which I have worked.

I am also grateful to a number of organizations whose invitations to speak to courses and conferences initially led me to formulate certain sections of this book, and to the members of those courses whose discussion and suggestions assisted me in shaping my ideas. These include the Department of Education and Science, the Manchester Education Committee, the Inner London Education Committee, and the Kent Education Committee. Amongst these conferences I have a special debt to those on the Organization and Management of Secondary Schools arranged by the Department of Education and Science in Wales. The skilful and exceptionally well-informed programmes of these inevitably led to especially profitable sessions. Parts of Chapter 9 are based on a talk broadcast by the BBC, *At Arms Length*, as well as a lecture given for the Advisory Centre for Education on a most interesting course.devised by Maurice Craft on *The Home and The School*.

I am especially grateful for the skilful and patient understanding of Jean Hardy, who typed the manuscript.

Although there are no books and almost no articles in periodicals which cover the subject of this book I am very grateful to a small number of books which do bear on aspects of school organization and school policy. These are at last beginning to provide data and comparisons for the teacher interested in this field. Full bibliographical details are given where specific reference is made to them, and I have included a list of helpful books which I recommend on page 100. I am grateful also to those authors and publishers who have kindly allowed me to quote extracts from their books.

M.M.

I

Introduction

For many teachers, and amongst them perhaps the most involved in their subject and sensitive to their pupils' needs, 'running things', 'organization', 'management' are boring and routine activities, which appear incompatible with a real liking for 'teaching'. In the three-stream school, both 'selective' by being a grammar school and selective by being 'non-selective', this didn't matter too much. There were few chores involved, curriculum innovation was an unnecessary term, and teachers were friends (or perhaps enemies) rather than 'colleagues'. An experienced teacher with a good qualification in his subject could be dubbed 'Senior Mathematics Master', the examination arrangements could be fixed up over coffee, and the new chap would probably learn from the atmosphere and a few friendly bits of off-the-cuff advice.

But every year we have now more large comprehensive schools, and the advertisements go out: 'Head of English Department, Scale 5, interest in all aspects of the subject, able to look after the school magazine [a newly reorganized school that – they'll soon learn that the Head of Department is not the right person!], and to lead a lively team [probably means a disparate group grudgingly brought together from three schools].' What ideas do the applicants have about the role of Head of Department? What assumptions are in the mind of the Head Teacher and interviewing body? Is there any need for job definition? Is there any special expertise? Is there any experience that can be codified and know-how that can be summed up for the aspiring Head of Department in a comprehensive school?

It is certain that the aims and approaches urgently required by a

Head of Department in the large comprehensive school are only partially seen by many of the applicants and LEA's alike. The tradition embodied in the early use of special responsibility allowances under the Burnham scale dies hard. This tradition gave extra money and status to the best qualified and frequently most 'senior' teacher of the subject. His position was associated primarily with teaching A-level; indeed there are many so-called Heads of Departments in grammar schools at the time that I write who teach *only* O- and A-level groups, and whose interest in the younger pupils is minimal. These teachers are now being faced with reorganization – and their experience and developed attitudes, their very competence and professional qualities, have given them little help towards the role required in the new school. It would be harsh to say that they have in many cases not 'earned' their often substantial allowances, but it would be accurate to say these have been more in the nature of general merit allowances than functional payments for specific tasks.

Many LEA's, now faced with creating a new school pattern, have a long history of distributing special responsibility allowances that has prepared the ground badly. The policy of these LEA's was to define a 'Department' in terms of the teaching of O- and A-levels in the subject, and even in some cases to rule that all the 'Departments' so created in any one school must be headed by teachers being paid the same grade. This resulted in such anomalies as the only Latin teacher receiving a Grade C allowance for 'leading' himself. It also served to perpetuate the approach that money was paid for seniority in a limited sense rather than for leadership, and thus at the time of reorganization there are protected holders of allowances with little experience or awareness of what they now have to face.

And if they should turn, as members of any profession may be expected to turn, to the shelves of the library, they will find virtually no guidance, even though their role is crucial for the schools we are creating. The nation has largely accepted, however grudgingly in some areas, a policy of creating a new type of school with insufficient detailed investigation into the organizational demands of such an institution![1] It has gradually become apparent

---

[1] Cf. Professor Boris Ford's report on the Bristol plans for secondary school reorganization for the *Bristol Evening Post*, 22 June 1965, in which he commented: 'There has been no attempt to set up comparative studies and research into the ways

that the understanding, skill, and energy of what might be called 'the middle management' are vital to a reasonable level of success. But where is the help for which applicants for and holders of such posts must look, the guidance which it can only too often be seen they need?

Looking at the educational scene more widely, it is obvious that the educational thinking of recent years has been largely at two divergent levels: ideas have been worked out either at the class level, between the individual teacher and his pupils, or at the broader community level of sociological investigation, only rarely narrowing down to the overall implications for a school. There is almost nothing in print about the departmental impact of educational advance. Yet the answer to the question that needs to be put about any curricula or educational innovation – 'How do you make it operational?' – is nearly always best answered in *departmental* terms. This is as true of the Cambridge non-linguistic classics project as it is of the Schools Council/Nuffield Humanities Curriculum Project. It is certainly true, I should forcefully argue, of the important trends in English teaching. To pinpoint a single example, you can't encourage the pupils of your class to read widely if the Head of Department operates a 'Set Book' issuing system.

Every school has some form of 'organization' and 'structure', however pompous a piece of jargon the terms may seem for the relaxed but efficient approaches of some smaller schools. The question is whether the organization helps the teacher, and thus the pupil, or not. I feel the Head of Department is responsible for creating the space, as it were, in which the subject can flourish,[1] and that his 'organization' is essential to produce the most effective, personal, and vigorous teaching of the subject to the best needs of the pupils.

In this book I hope to be able to give some sort of help to the teacher considering the post of Head of Department, and at least

[1] I owe this phrase to John Davies of the Department of Education at York University.

the schools have been working. . . . Compared with the planning and production of a supersonic aircraft, the development of the comprehensive school in Bristol has gone forward with astonishingly little detailed study, research, experiment, testing, re-designing which would have seemed essential in so large a project; though compared with other comprehensive schemes, Bristol has not been unduly backward in this respect – just typically backward.'

to make it possible for him to start off on his own initiative, and not, as so many new Heads of Departments have to, be always coping with yesterday's problems today, and rarely able to get an overall perspective, or feel he is moving forward on a reasonably firm strategy, one in which 'flexibility' is a virtue, not merely a euphemism for muddle.

Naturally, and I hope profitably, I shall be speaking out my own experience, firstly at Abbey Wood School, a mixed comprehensive school of about 1,200 in an almost exclusively working-class area, and secondly at Crown Woods School, which is also mixed, but which takes a larger number of pupils (about 2,000) and has a considerably more comprehensive range of pupils, both socially and intellectually. Before writing this book, I gave up, regretfully, my department and became 'Director of Studies' at Crown Woods School; this is a post with general oversight, in close collaboration with the Headmaster and Deputy Headmistress, of the curriculum, placing pupils in teaching groups, and devising of the timetable. From this position, and my later one as a Headmaster, I have naturally looked at the role of Head of Department in a somewhat different light, but this experience has confirmed and amplified my conviction that the work of the larger school depends above all on the grasp of their roles by the Heads of Departments, their ability to create the appropriate departmental environment for the teachers and their skill in encouraging an atmosphere in which ideas are drawn out, fostered, and developed.

My own specialism has been English, and my personal practical experience of leading a department has been in the context of that subject. The crucial points, though, are, I am convinced, not limited to one subject or group of subjects. Certainly each subject discipline has its especial aspects and the work of leading, say, a craft department would feel very different from that of a Modern Languages department; nevertheless, the essential points remain, and I have taken many of my examples from my personal experience. I have, however, also drawn on a wide range of observations of other schools and other departments. I am thinking most of the time of the 'all through' comprehensive of 1,200 to 2,000 pupils, but the central theme, and most of the application applies to 'Middle Schools', 'Junior High Schools', and 'Senior High Schools', for the whole of secondary education today demands the emergence of the new type of Head of Department. That is not to

say, of course, that many of the concepts of departmental procedure and attitude worked out for the larger school aren't also
highly relevant to much smaller ones. It is also important to
realize that although not all that I recommend can be carried out
in the smaller departments of large schools, the kind of co-
operation described is just as important. Indeed, the Head of
Department possibly has an even stronger duty in such circumstances to initiate co-operative procedures. Young teachers, for
instance, need even more careful support when there are fewer of
them.

There are four main difficulties in trying to write the kind of
account that I consider would be helpful, and they are difficulties
which are so considerable as to make one wonder whether it is
possible:

In the first place, and obviously, schools differ. The new Head of
Department holds his position in a particular school, different
from those which I have observed and in which I have had my
experience, and different, in all probability, from the ones in
which the new Head of Department has had his earlier experience.
It will, I suspect, prove impossible to write without conveying the
impression that schools are more nearly similar than they in fact
are. The way pupils walk along corridors, the methods by which
stock is ordered, the care put into keeping the lavatories clean, the
tenor of staff discussion – all the trivia of school life will affect
every decision the Head of Department makes, and throughout
my book it needs to be understood that my examples are no more
than examples of the kinds of actions which should be taken.

On the other hand, various, and obviously central, Head-of-
Department responsibilities are not particular to the large
school. If one is to describe all a Head of Department is expected
to carry out, and all in equal detail, one risks stating the obvious
and listing points which are clear to any newcomer. Yet if one
leaves out those parts of the role that do not differ from school to
school, one risks misplacing the emphasis.

There is then the difficulty of talking about a subject department
without talking about actual teaching. One of my central theses is
that the *kind* as well as the quality of the subject teaching in a
school depends on the way the Head of Department *manages* his
team. It is therefore very difficult to talk about the management
without talking about the teaching. But I want to try. I want to

show that theories and attitudes to the teaching of particular subjects in isolation are not enough: the departmental framework needs adjusting to implement these theories.

Lastly, there is the difficulty of which I am most actually aware: of keeping the reality, of conveying something of the atmosphere of a school in my outline of words. What may seem straightforward on paper can be a considerable achievement in the hectic flurry of a term. The immense difficulties of managing things well in a school need remembering. As I shall discuss in detail in Chapter 7, schools are badly equipped and teachers are poorly serviced. Anyone who has his own children at school will know of the numerous minor inefficiencies that beset their days, inefficiencies that are cumulatively serious. With the lowest auxiliary-to-professional ratio of any profession, with such dismally poor office equipment (phones, typewriters, reprographic equipment), and in many instances such ludicrous accommodation, the reality of management and leadership for many Heads of Departments is a nightmare. Headmastering may be the art of the possible – but leading a department in a large secondary school is often the art of the impossible. I think some of my points will help newcomers to cope, but I do not underestimate the difficulties of putting ideas into practice. I do not apologize for a large number of what may seem trivial details, for the success of the large ambition of comprehensive education (as indeed the success of the large ambitions of many modern curricula developments) depends firmly on the grasp of a mass of detail.

*   *   *   *

Perhaps an account of the work of a Head of Department in a comprehensive school cannot be said to have a coherent argument, but it has a recurrent theme: the Head of Department has to isolate what I take to be the two key factors of this kind of school, and to regard them not as problems to be fought, but as strengths to be exploited. These key factors are variety and size.

It is worth pondering on the implication of both. A three-stream grammar school is relatively homogenous in a number of ways, and has a strong tendency towards ever greater homogeneity. The large comprehensive school has a diversity which is quite staggering in comparison with the comparative simplicity of

most individual teachers' backgrounds and experience from school
to further education and back. There is firstly the variety of pupil
ability, background, and interest. There is no possibility of re-
maining stuck, for instance, with a Platonic vision of the ideal
Sixth-Former – there is every possible kind of person jostling in
the sixth. Perhaps less often realized, or at least openly discussed,
is the variety of teachers. A grammar school staff-room especially
tended towards a norm: it is impossible to pretend this is so in the
comprehensive staff. There are other manifestations of variety as
well – of especial significance is the variety of educational ambition. What the school hopes to be able to do for its pupils is very
varied indeed: the boy going at sixteen to be a chef, the girl going
at eighteen to a College of Education; the pupil interested in
puppets and the pupil who goes about surveying – no one educational aim will fit.

And size is not simple either. It starts with the size of building
or campus, which may require a lengthy walk to traverse, and
which brings with it problems of communication, storage, tired-
ness, but which allows flexibility. The number of pupils needs
looking at from various points of view, but for the moment
perhaps I could just note that, for instance, the Head of Mathematics in a school of 2,000 may have seventy-five teaching groups
for which he is responsible; or put another way Mathematics is
taught in any one week for perhaps 375 periods. Obviously the
teaching staff numbers are similarly high: his department may
include, say, twelve full-time teachers and four or five part-time
ones. Then there is the size of the stock of equipment and teaching
materials within the department. As Head of English I had some
16,000 books (not to mention duplicated sheets, gramophone
records, tapes, slides, etc.). Possibly that figure conveys the real
size of a comprehensive school more than the bare statement of
roll.

In this situation it is essential to think big – especially to see
what these two factors of variety and size can offer. I think most
people find that the situation is not one in which the tasks are
merely the old ones writ large – the central nature of the post is
different from that in a smaller school. There would, for instance,
be little accuracy in the old title 'Senior French Master' – the 'Head
of the French Department' is quite a different post.

I hope to show in the course of the book in what way it differs,

to make it clear why the department in a large comprehensive
school has such a very different feel to that in a smaller segregated
school. The difference, it will be found, is qualitative and not
simply quantitative.

A general instance is needed at this point: many of the tasks
traditionally associated with the job of Headmaster will devolve
on to the Head of Department. In this transfer the tasks will be
transformed, often becoming more active and more detailed.
The Incorporated Association of Assistant Masters in Secondary
Schools (I.A.A.M.) put it well in the second edition of their book
on the comprehensive school when they said:

> In 1959 members attending our conferences impressed on us
> that a comprehensive school is as good as its Headmaster. We
> would amend that in the light of our 1965 conferences to
> 'A comprehensive school is as good as its leadership'. The
> leadership now more clearly includes those who rank as
> Assistant Masters but who might well be called Assistant Head-
> masters.[1]

The teaching strength of a comprehensive school is the strength
of its departments; the pleasure of teaching in a comprehensive
school (and it can be a real pleasure) is the pleasure of those two
factors, size and variety, in the setting of a departmental team.
The central aim of the Head of Department is to foster this team,
to develop a complementary unity and diversity; common
ground and sub-specialisms. It is a formidable task, in which the
Head of Department must constantly remind himself that his time
and concentration are required for *people* (whether teachers or
pupils), and that helping people give of their best is what 'administration' means.

*   *   *   *

I shall consider the job of Head of Department in detail in relation
to nine aspects of responsibility (in Chapters 2–11). I have risked
listing the trivial detail and making the small suggestion because
such minor points, though they can sometimes seem ludicrous in
cold print, are ideas which many people's experience has suggested
are helpful – and which, though they can be rejected, should be

[1] *Teaching in Comprehensive Schools, A Second Report*, C.U.P., 1967.

known about in advance, and not discovered on the job. First, though, as an overview, I'd like to quote the reactions of a group of experienced U.S. researchers. We are, naturally, used to the ways in which we run our schools. It is therefore valuable to share for a moment the findings of outsiders. In 1967 the U.S. National Council of Teachers of English sponsored (as a follow-up to an earlier National Study in America), *A Study of the Teaching of English in Selected British Secondary Schools*.[1] One of the features of these schools that most impressed these visitors was the leadership of the departments. One of the implications for American schools which they noted was that 'appointing a department chairman for the leadership he can bring rather than for his length of service in the school can do much to vitalize the English program'.[2] This is true across the subjects of the school, as is their placing of the Head of Department's difficulties and necessary abilities:

The English chairman operates with as much or as little authority as the headmaster will allow. His role is peculiar in that it is highly prized, carries with it a stipend of as much as one-third more than that paid a regular teacher, yet frequently permits him no direct authority over his own teachers. Indeed after completing a year's probationary teaching, individual teachers are awarded a tenure-like condition which is virtually unbreakable. The department chairman, who often works with the headmaster in the selection and assignment of teachers, can, and often does, write the syllabus for his department. But whether it is followed or not is a matter of chance and the personality of the chairman. There is nothing in his role which assures compliance.

Even so, the strength of English chairman in both England and Scotland was noted by all observers. In overall assessments they ranked the competence of the English chairman second only to the overall quality of the faculty among special strengths, citing his unique abilities in two-thirds of the institutions visited. Again and again observers commented on the energy and vision of the chairman, his commitment to the larger professional scene, his participation in outside professional activity, his presence as the 'driving force behind curriculum

[1] U.S. Department of Health, Education and Welfare, 1968.
[2] Ibid, p 113. *Department chairman* is the U.S. term for Head of Department.

revision in the school', his close relationship with the head-master, his receptivity to new ideas from the staff.

The English chairman operates as a professional and intellec-tual leader within the school because he is selected for this purpose.[1]

In this book I shall consider how the 'energy and vision' can be applied. It is one of a series designed to explore in some detail the possibilities and problems in the organization of secondary schools today. Like the others, this book is complete in itself, but a number of the themes touched on (e.g. pastoral care, the processes of decision making) are taken up in greater detail in other books in the series.

[1] Ibid, p. 93.

2

The Complementary Team

Interest in a particular school subject may be the starting-point of a valuable teaching career, but it is not sufficient for a Head of Department. The vision that informs his activity is not the first instance particular to his subject: it is the vision of a group of teachers, the department team. I used the phrase 'complementary unity and diversity' earlier. This, I should suggest, is the starting-point.

There may be as many as fourteen teachers working in the field of Science or English, or as few as three or four in Classics or Music, but in both cases the individual must function as an organic grouping. They must, if at all possible, have a common point of view. If one French teacher considers the only justification for teaching the subject is to familiarize pupils with the culture and background of the country, and another that it is primarily a training to improve understanding of the workings of language (and this divergence can easily be found) the department will not function. *This* degree of diversity completely fractures the necessary unity of the teaching team, so that a pupil whose class happens to be taught by Mr X will be exposed to virtually a different subject to that experienced by a pupil in Mrs Y's group. A common ground is essential, but this is not to expect members of a department to be carbon copies one of the other. The Head of Department will welcome a creative diversity within the common broad attitude, and, this is my major point, he will especially look out for sub-specialisms. That one music teacher has a special zest for medieval and renaissance music, or another is particularly strong in the field of folk music and its contemporary performance, is a valuable divergence that can be exploited to strengthen the comprehensive power of the team. But if one teacher believes that the starting-point for musical experience is a definition of note values whereas a parallel class are plunged into listening and creating improvised music, the observer can be sure that the overall benefit to pupils is far lower than it should be.

A common viewpoint is, then, the Head of Department's first aim, and he will realize that it cannot be simply imposed on his team. The most fundamental reason for this is that any satisfactory approach to a subject is likely to be gathered from the observation and experience of a number of people, and wisdom is not going to be the monopoly of a single person. But there is, of course, a complementary point: no one is willing to take on the philosophy of another, simply handed out as instructions. Even if he were, the effect would most probably be unsatisfactory, for it is difficult to put into action satisfactorily the ideas of others. Far more conviction is put into the effort if each individual is identified with the ideas, and can feel both part of them and that they are part of him.

Appointments

In establishing a department with a shared viewpoint, there are two major efforts to be made: one is in creating a climate of discussion (the subject of Chapter 3), and the other is the selecting and appointing of staff. Whatever the right balance of responsibility in the smaller (say three-form entry) school, it is quite clear that the Head of Department must have a major, if not *the* major, say in the appointing of new teachers to his department. On the one hand he is best fitted to judge whether the applicant's qualities are within the broad approach to the subject of *this* department, and on the other it is the Head of Department who (as I shall discuss on page 31) has the responsibility of inducting the new teacher, guiding him, and helping his establishment in the new community.

It may be objected that to expect Heads of Departments to take a large part in the selection and appointment of teachers could encourage them merely to buttress their own positions by searching for those who will too easily agree with them. In practice this is not to be feared (certainly no more than that the advice of a Head Teacher will produce an undesirable choice of Heads of Departments). The Head of Department should at the very least provide notes on the application forms, and make recommendations for the short-list of candidates. He or she may be insufficiently experienced as yet to have the full responsibility for the often tedious and confusing task of sifting application forms. (It is difficult to weigh qualifications and experience, and assess additional statements.) In any case, the initial application forms do not usually provide the information about attitudes to the subject which is the especial province of the Head of Department. It seems to me that this first process could be done by any experienced person – it is not a specifically departmental decision. However, after the drawing-up of the short-list, the Head of Department has, I maintain, a sensitive and important task: to assess each of the candidates from three points of view: member of the departmental team, able to share and contribute, join in and diverge; competent, reliable, and sympathetic teacher; and, lastly, member of the school community. Undoubtedly the ideal next move is to invite the short-list applicants, preferably but not necessarily singly, to visit the school informally.[1] Such a visit is an opportunity for the Head of Department to get to know the applicant by exposing him or her to aspects of the school and department, and to inquire of other senior members of the department their opinions. Half a day, plus lunch, is probably sufficient for the applicant to have a good talk with the Head of Department, to meet separately another, perhaps younger, member of the department whom he can question, to visit a couple of classes, and to be shown round the school by a pupil. Controversial points can be aired; ideas explained; the atmosphere sampled. And later the Head of Department can collate his own impressions with that of his colleagues, and with the applicant's wishes and opinions. This is a reasonable basis for making a recommendation to the Headmaster for the final formal interview. It will be seen that such a series of meetings have a complementary advantage: the applicant is given a better chance to decide whether he wants to go ahead with his application – for a successful appointment requires a two-way wish. In some departments the process will be carried a stage further by the Head of Department being invited to attend

[1] I appreciate that mean and outmoded expense arrangements frequently make this difficult.

the formal interview as the key 'expert witness' whose questions, reactions, and summing up will be of crucial, though not necessarily overwhelming, weight. It would be a rash Head Teacher and Board of Governors that would fly in the face of a strong reaction – especially an unfavourable one. An alien voice, with a strong new point of view, may be needed by a particular department at a particular time, but if this is the opinion of the Headmaster it should be expressed clearly well in advance of the appointment, and discussed with the Head of Department. On most occasions, though, the voice of the leader, who will have to work with the new applicant, and reconcile his or her ideas, personality, and teaching approaches, is the voice that should be strongest.

Appointing staff is not a passive job – it is rare for a department to be well staffed if the machinery of public advertisement is the only method applied, and that mechanically. The wise Head of Department starts with a careful relationship with all his present teachers so that the possibilities of resignation are well known. A surprise resignation should almost never occur; the Head of Department will be looking to the long-term needs of the department *and* to the career prospects of his team. In many cases such a close link is repaid by an advance resignation, which can allow the school to advertise at a better time.

Word of an impending advertisement, and of the kind of person being sought, can then be sent to the University Appointment Boards, any Colleges of Education whose approach is known to be broadly sympathetic to the school's own, and to any individual known to the school and Head of Department. The aims is not, of course, to by-pass public advertisement, which would be both unwise and unethical, but to supplement by personal contact.

The gap between sending off an application form and hearing that one has or has not been short-listed is unpleasant for candidates – and often so long that they take another job in the meantime. It is important to ensure that all applications are acknowledged, and that the short-list invitations then go out as soon as possible. It is worth enclosing a standard duplicated description of the school, together with a special piece on the department and this particular job: the more the candidate knows in advance, the more profitable and realistic the informal meeting I mentioned earlier.

It is now widely accepted by many people (except a number of administrators who can point to filled vacancies and ask what there is to worry about) that the finding, appointing, and recruiting of staff is inefficient and discourteous. The Head of Department can often mitigate this. His trouble will be repaid by well-filled posts.

The Complementary Team

The size of a department in a comprehensive school allows a deliberate policy of creating a diversity, a *complementary* diversity, within the overall unity. As much, for instance, as one admires the single Art teacher in a three-form-entry grammar school, one is forced to realize that the impossible is being asked of one teacher: to add to the skills of a basic Art teacher special interest in graphic design, pottery, three-dimensional work, stage designing, the history of art. Some area or areas must be mastered less than adequately. The Head of Department in a comprehensive school, on the other hand, can survey the full scope of his subjects and ensure that his appointments bring in the range of what could be called sub-specialisms. He may specifically advertise with this in mind, and although it is unlikely that he will sacrifice the better applicant to the right sub-specialism, he will probably be able to maintain the balance. Thus a Geography Department will have one member who is a specialist keenly interested in urban geography and town-planning, another whose special sphere is geology, and a third whose interest in geography is veering very close to sociology.

In English teaching, the needs for such sub-specialism are every bit as strong. The lingering notion that saying 'every teacher is a teacher of English' (a notion which recent research has confirmed – though not perhaps in the sense it was originally meant[1]) is the same as saying that 'every teacher can teach timetabled English equally well' is ridiculous, and the demands for specialized knowledge and techniques have grown enormously. It is this tired belief in the essential amateurism of teaching English that keeps out of the classroom, or weakens the effectiveness of, many aspects of our work long agreed in general principle. It is twelve years since the tape-recorder, for instance, was heralded as a valuable aid – yet

[1] Cf. *Language, the Learner and the School*, especially Part One, by Douglas Barnes et al., Penguin Books, 1969.

how infrequently and how feebly is it used. It was in 1935, to take another example, that Raymond O'Malley first wrote[1] of the work that needs to be done in the analysis of reaction to advertisements – yet how few pupils really have the guidance needed. Screen Education, to take a disgraceful example, dates back to the days of Stanley Reed's (later Director of the British Film Institute) teaching in East Ham, and its importance was clearly confirmed by the Newsom report's plea: 'We should wish to add a strong claim for the study of film and television in their own right.'[2] But the work done now is pitifully rare. No doubt the reason is partly concerned with the practical difficulties (which I shall discuss in Chapter 7), but even more significant is the shortage of specialized *knowledge*.

The need for specialized approaches can be met, and the relevant knowledge made available to the team as a whole, by judicious appointments.

But the need to feed specialist knowledge into the team is not the only reason for pursuing a policy of sub-specialists. Firstly, the department needs adequate theory of the subject as a secondary school activity, and this needs articulating into a practical policy. This, even if it were desirable, is too huge an undertaking for one person, but on the other hand it doesn't come from vague general discussion alone. This discussion needs prompting, informing, and summing up by the sub-specialists, who each in their own way can be relied upon to be in close touch with ideas elsewhere, to read the relevant journals, attend courses, study the new educational publications in their particular field – in fact to *lead* the department. Only with a team many of whom are working in this way can the broader policy of a department be based on adequately detailed foundations.

Secondly, such a structuring of what I like to call a 'complementary team' allows the more narrow administration to be delegated in a satisfactory and meaningful way, and for the admittedly difficult to distribute and somewhat irrational 'responsibility allowances' to be used according to a reasonable, positive, and acceptable pattern. A large organization inevitably requires a large quantity of sheer chores – indeed they increase with the size

[1] In *The Quality of Education*, edited by Denys Thompson and James Reeves, Frederick Muller, 1935; still a seminal book on many aspects of secondary teaching.
[2] *Half our Future*, H.M.S.O., 1963, para. 474.

of school according to a geometric and not an arithmetical progression. It is tempting but, as I have already submitted, quite wrong, for the Head of Department to see himself as the 'ideas man', and to expect various of his teachers to undertake the organizing of the schemes. One Head of Department of a large comprehensive school, when questioned at the end of a talk in which he explained his work, was asked, 'What, then, are the duties of your Deputy?' 'Oh,' was the answer, 'he is really my secretary.' I should offer as a guiding principle an opposing theory of delegation: 'No chores without ideas.' In other words, as far as is possible link the admittedly many and admittedly complex chores with the associated professional excitements – that is the ideas, the keeping-up-to-date, the planning, leading, being an expert. I have known departments in which teachers are called upon to 'Check this list, please', 'Do the daily substitution for absent teachers', 'Organize the booking of the hall and library', 'Do the departmental stock order'. If these solid doses of undiluted organization are ladled out with no organic connection to their related ideas, there is inefficiency (for such tasks are normally done more accurately by the person to whom their success means most), dissatisfaction, and frustration.[1]

If this principle is accepted, the Head of Department will start looking at his team of teachers in a different light: they are a complementary group, each having something in common – a broad agreement about the subject approaches – but each, or many, being differentiated by being the acknowledged leader in a particular field. Immediately a third advantage reveals itself: the huge hierarchy of a large school can be daunting to a young teacher, and the points of decision making, of public recognition, of influencing others, may seem very remote. In theory the channels of communication are open to all: through the discussion of a department meeting (which I shall discuss in the next chapter)

[1] Cf. 'It had always been my intention that the Deputy Head should be more in the nature of a partner, or a second or alternative Head, than an assistant to the Head in the way that a Senior Mistress or a Deputy Head in a small school often is. . . . This means that instead of the less important things being discussed by the Deputy and the more important by the Head, the division must be in other ways; there must be specific matters of equal importance, some of which are done by the Deputy and some by the Head.'
Margaret Miles, *Comprehensive Schooling*, Longman, 1968.
This is the essential point about delegation and applies equally at departmental level.

the individual's views are sifted, brought together, and made known to the Heads of Departments' meeting – and thus in the fullness of time influence overall school thinking. I don't want to deride this process; it can work, and indeed it is up to the Head of Department to make sure that it does work by fidelity to his team's views, and concise but convincing exposition to the Heads of Departments' meeting and Head Teacher. However, it is also important to recognize that the 'junior' teacher needs more than this. He needs to feel he has an especial place of his own over and above his classroom teaching, especially after, say, his first year when his attention is not exclusively taken up with his own classes. To give as many staff as possible some such responsibility (the responsibilities will vary, of course, in weight and significance) is to give each a feeling of having a special place in the school, one in which he or she is the acknowledged leader. The ill effects of not following this policy as far as possible can usually be seen both in staff turnover and in meagreness of subject thinking. A vicious circle can be created in which the department can be seen to have no direction or meaningful policy; the Head of Department might offer as a defence the point that staff don't stay long enough to create a 'climate of discussion' (such as I describe in Chapter 3). But the outsider can see that the first difficulty leads to the second, which in its turn certainly makes the first worse. This is an apparently unbreakable vicious circle – unless a well-defined responsibility for an interesting aspect of the work can be placed in a teacher's hands. He is then committed to the department for he has a stake in its future.

Such a view of the department breaks up the linear hierarchy, which is an unpleasant feature of many large organizations, and substitutes, as it were, a confederate structure. The actual Burnham 'responsibility allowances', are used as the label suggests, for specific and acknowledged 'responsibilities' (in which ideas, knowledge, leadership of others, and organization are combined). I like to think of each of these people as 'Advisers' to the rest of the team, and the Deputy Head of Department, apart from being clearly a potential Head of Department and able to lead the team during any illness or absence of the Head, as a special Adviser having *specific spheres of interest and responsibility*. The sub-specialisms which might be appropriate for an actual department are clearly not of equal importance, and can be linked in any number

of combinations. Here is a way of building up an English departmental advisory team:

Drama: (I prefer to think of dramatic work as an integral part of
the whole range of 'English', and I therefore do not like a separate
drama department.) Such a person would not necessarily teach
more drama or take much more of the extra-curricula dramatic
activities, but he would have the expertise and enthusiasm to put
at the disposal of the team. This would include practical flair, a
wide knowledge of plays (most essential), as well as some historical knowledge. He would advise on classroom drama, ensure
that it flourishes in all the classes, plan the extra-curricula work
(see Chapter 10), give close personal encouragement to the public
productions, and handle all the associated administration (booking halls, ordering equipment and books, organizing publicity,
and so on).

The Screen: that is television and film, as two linked interests. All
the teachers will have some interest, but one person at least must
have a wide knowledge of the film and television repertoire,
techniques, organization, and critical approaches. In addition, he
should ideally have some film-making skill.

The Mass Media: as a whole, or simply the Press and advertisements. Somewhere in the departmental team there should be at
least one person who has some detailed knowledge of mass communications and current thinking from both the practitioner's and
the critic's point of view.

Sound/Tape: whether or not the school has (as I argue in Chapter 7
it should have) a central recording studio, it is valuable to have at
least one teacher who combines a knowledge of tape-recorders
and sound studio techniques with an appreciation and interest in
sound as an art and communication medium. Such a teacher can
at the least guide uncertain colleagues in the technicalities of the
tape-recorder, but more than that he can lead the development of
teaching techniques. He is likely to draw his colleagues' attention
to particularly significant radio programmes . . . and so on. (This
is an interest that might well combine with drama or screen, but if
so it tends to be the least favoured aspect: let it therefore stand on
its own.)

Student Teachers: I shall discuss the department's responsibilities to student teachers more fully in Chapter 8. Relevant here, though, is the notion that although each teacher (after his probationary year) must have a sympathetic grasp of the real training needs of students, it is valuable if one member of the department at least has thought closely about the training of teachers, is familiar with the training institutions (cf. page 69), and can be known as a specialist in this sphere.

Examinations: The various external examinations have their own expertise and problems – as well as a fair load of basic administration (ordering set books, completing entry forms, assembling projects, organizing orals). It is worth considering asking one person to look after the needs of sixth form, and a second the 'first level' O- or C.S.E. examinations. Obviously this principle will not only hold good if and when this pattern of external examinations changes but will be even more important, for new examinations are a strain on teachers to assimilate.

In certain schools A-level is normally thought of as the province of the Head of Department – but in certain situations it would be wiser to ask another teacher to have oversight of the A-level work, which is, after all, specialized, numerically limited in extent, and requires a careful eye keeping on texts, co-ordination of teachers, stocking of the library, and so on. In a comprehensive school, even with a large number of candidates studying for A-level, it is arguable that the main energy and direction of the Head of Department is likely to be dispersed elsewhere. The time when the most specialized advanced work was equated inevitably with leadership of the department is, I think, going. Without in any way reducing the care and effort given to advanced candidates, it would be possible to have their needs looked after by someone other than the Head of Department, and this might, incidentally, change the inevitability of a graduate always holding the Head of Department post.

The introduction of C.S.E., and its rapid spread, taken together with the raising of the school leaving age in 1973, has led to huge numbers of fifth-year examination candidates, increased in many schools by the large number of less-able Sixth-Formers still after a 'first-level' qualification. It is usually wise to have an 'Adviser' for this work, especially as C.S.E. has presented challenge to the teacher beyond those of the more limited O-level. In English, for instance, the range of 'set books' or 'recommended books' is very wide, and of these include books with which many teachers will not be familiar. (Here is an example of the administrative – the problems of ordering, circulating, co-ordinating – linking with the educational – the reading, choosing, recommending to other teachers.) Then there are the 'project' or 'course work' considerations, with teachers often needing a focus for discussion, and the complexities of an oral element. A school of 2,000 might well be entering 250 candidates for C.S.E. (and a further 100 for O-level) in one summer – the needs of the teachers working with them are probably best met by a C.S.E. Adviser as I have described.

The 'hierarchy' of a department takes on a different feel if the appointments are made in this way, and responsibilities delegated to some such pattern. Instead of a vertical pattern, which follows Deputy with 'Third in the Department', there is rather a horizontal pattern, which I have roughly indicated in the diagram below.

Co-ordinators:

| Head | Deputy |

Advisers:

| Students | Screen: film and tv | Examinations with special reference to C.S.E. | Sound recording | Less able pupils | Drama |

Teachers with no special responsibilities:

| | | | | |

Perhaps an even better way of looking at the responsibilities would be to think of a many-sided figure, which can be looked at according to the aspect under consideration, so that different people come to 'the top' at different times. Such sub-specialisms would be arranged with a considerable degree of flexibility, and from year to year there might be some interchange, e.g. moving from the bookstall to pupil publications. This not only increases the department's total knowledge, it also gives greater freedom for teachers to choose their area of concern, and to tackle something new from time to time:

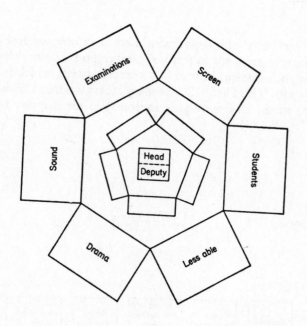

Opposite is an example of a copy (with fictitious names of teachers) of an actual list of responsibilities for a particular English department one year:

ENGLISH DEPARTMENT RESPONSIBILITIES 1969/70

Audio-visual including all aspects of film, film
    visits, library resources, contact with
    Audio-Visual Aids Assistant and use of
    reprographic facilities - Miss Jones
Book suggestions. Verse and Prose (including
    reading lists) - Mrs Stephens. Drama - Mr
    Smith
Book borrowing - Mrs Grace
Book Shop - Mr Brown and Mrs Furman (Tuesdays
    and Fridays)
Broadcasting and advising on sound and use of
    tape-recorders - Mr Cooper
C.S.E. including advice to pupils and teachers
    and all fifth year examination entries - Mr
    Smith
Displays - Mrs Fox
Drama including advising teachers on classroom
    drama and co-ordinating productions - Mr
    Smith
Drama groups - 1st year - Mr Edwards and Miss
                    Arnold (Mondays)
                    2nd year - Miss Mosely
                    (Thursdays)
                    3rd and 4th years - Mr Holder
                    (Fridays)
                    5th, 6th and 7th year - Mr Smith
                    (Tuesdays)
Equipment repairs (tape-recorder, record player,
    etc.) - Mr Cooper
Film Society - Miss Jones (Wednesdays)
Hall and drama room bookings - Mr Smith
Internal examinations   3rd year -
                    Miss Manley
                    4th year -
                    Miss Jones
                    5th year -
                    Mr Smith
                    6th and 7th year -
                    Mrs Winick
Lighting for drama productions - Miss Jones

Minutes of department meetings - Miss Arnold
POD magazine - Mr Penton

Prizes and Sixth Form Literary Competition -
   Miss Jones

Public examination entries for all 6th and 7th
   years except C.S.E. - Miss Jones

Record cards - Mrs Winick

Shadow timetable - Mrs Winick

Stationery - Mrs Grace

Students including advising teacher-tutors -
   Miss Moseley

Theatre visits - Mr Smith

An obvious point, but one often overlooked, is that the responsibilities must be clearly known to the department itself, and to many others in the school; hence a duplicated list such as this.

The spheres of responsibilities will vary widely from department to department according to subjects, but also, of course, from school to school even in the same subject departments. The principle, though, is the same, and it is one which is essential for the health of a department: let as many people as possible share the 'creative' work of searching for educational ideas and teaching material, link this with the related chores or organization and administration, and thus build up a complementary team with a diversity of special interest within a unity of broad approach – but such a unity depends on a climate of discussion.

3

A Climate of Discussion

You will often hear that 'It all depends on personalities', and that 'human contacts' are the most important aspects of education. It is frequently implied that these are realities the large school insensitively ignores, or at best is impotent to foster. This is not so. However, human relationships need a suitable environment, and the Head of Department must consciously plan to encourage his team to work *as* a team, one in which individuality is honoured, yet is fed by the ideas and attitudes of others also. The most important element in this, and the element which can most fully be worked at by the Head of Department is the creating of what I shall call a 'climate of discussion'. I stress 'creating' because, although there is an element of luck depending on the particular characteristics of the teaching team, deliberate action can be taken over quite small matters to prompt discussion, to give it substance and direction, and to lead it towards action.

I almost feel like saying that it all depends on where the tea is made and who drinks it together. At any rate the starting-point is where the Head of Department spends his time during breaks and lunch hours – those very intensive and psychologically important times in school – and whether he is cut off from his team during these informal, relaxed times or not. Almost no schools have adequate staff accommodation, and the need for a 'Departmental Headquarters' – a materials and ideas base – in the large-team comprehensive schools has been recognized too late for the majority of actual buildings.[1] If, though, the Head of Department

[1] Cf. Department of Education and Science, 'Sixth Form and Staff', *Building Bulletin No. 25*, H.M.S.O., 1965.

has been provided, as many are, with a tiny room, and he then squeezes his Deputy a desk in one corner, it is vital that the two of them don't lurk there continuously, brewing up at break, and missing the to-and-fro of casual chat. A Head of Department must be easily available when his teachers are around (keeping, as far as possible, desk and paper work for the evening). Only by taking care over this will he be part of the informal communication network. Departments in which this simple action is not practised are characterized by 'unexpected' resignations, misconceived plans, and a remoteness that mitigates against cohesion. People are the first call on a departmental Head's time.

The corollary of this, though, is a subtler point: the possibility of informal chat over tea that is afforded by some departmental headquarters – especially for the more obviously 'specialized' departments (e.g. P.E., Craft, Science, Music) – can lead to the misapprehension that the morning tea break conversation has covered the necessary ground. It won't have done: informal chat is no substitute for the second piece of the departmental scheme: regular formal meetings with agendas and minutes. These are the crucial times when the department feels its strength, is aware of its weaknesses, and distils from its informal day-to-day talk a firm direction.

But such a meeting is always (and here I feel confident enough to be dogmatic) fruitless unless it draws on the informal discussion I have stressed so far and a whole series of minor strategies. I shall therefore describe these first, and then return to the subject of the formal meetings.

The Head of Department must know what goes on in the classes for which he is responsible. He needs to know for practical reasons (the provision of teaching material), for educational reasons (to see what aspects of the subject or approaches to learning are experienced by the pupils), to assist him in the spread of ideas, and to get to know the work of individual teachers. The teaching record book, although it has something of an old-fashioned, indeed an authoritarian air, seems to me an important foundation tool for the unity of a department. Looked at in context, some form of record book can be seen to serve a real purpose in maintaining the flow of basic information. The notes can be, in fact should be, very brief: a line for the 'material' of the lesson, an indication of the approaches, and a note of the homework set. The Head of Department will want to see those books more frequently than each term, but less often than weekly – each month seems about right.

The record book, of course, is a bare outline: for mutual comprehension frequent visiting of each other's lessons by as many as possible is important. The large school has been one of the most powerful forces in breaking down the quite terrifying older isolation of the individual teacher in his classroom. In the first school in which I taught, one well-established figure, whose voice was that of the conservative element in each of the staff, declared firmly, 'No one's been in my classroom for forty years – and they're not starting now!' Such an attitude may seem archaic today, but it is only by patient encouragement that the Head of Department can make the *mutual* visiting of lessons a relaxed and frequent part of the teaching pattern. It must grow from 'Have you anything interesting you'd like to show me?', rather than 'I'd like to see how you're getting on', but care is needed lest the young teacher gets the impression that only the unusual in his classroom is respected and worth looking at. Various small moves can make the visiting of a lesson less dramatic. It is especially helpful if routine visits for specific purposes can be made, e.g. if the Head of Department visits each first-year group to introduce himself, welcome the class, talk a little about the range of extra-curricula activities – and end by a promise to visit them during a lesson to see how they are getting on. Somewhat similarly, I should almost always personally introduce a new teacher to a class he or she is taking over.

Any team-teaching exercises, whatever their wider function in the teaching of the subject, and however modest they may be, serve to break the individual teacher's isolation, and to make clear the benefits of sharing work and observing each other. For instance, if three classes are brought together to see a film extract, and one of the teachers introduces it and initiates the questioning at the end, the visiting of classrooms later will not seem so strange. The pattern of work with students (which I discuss in Chapter 8) can be similarly helpful. Certainly, both informal discussion and formal meeting are enriched if those taking part know something of each other's work with actual pupils in actual run-of-the-mill teaching situations.

There are two mundane practical devices that need mentioning both because they can contribute positively to the climate of discussion, and also because, negatively but most importantly, they can sieve out of discussions the details of administration: they are the notice-board and the duplicated circular. A well-kept notice-board (with a 'Today' section scrupulously cleared each evening) is essential for all larger, and probably most smaller, departments. As well as routine announcements, reminders of forthcoming deadlines for reports and other scheduled events, details of interesting courses, and so forth, such a board will gather to it cuttings, suggestions, and queries from teachers that feed the department's thought.

And circulars? A good working rule is that anything that needs remembering by *each* teacher (e.g. examination marking arrangements, new books available, or dates of drama events) is best put on a circular so that it can be carried around for reference. All announcements and all administrative detail should be disseminated by notice or circular, and not by meeting, unless discussion or subtle explanation is needed (and even then the details should be confirmed in a circular). It is a waste of time, a misuse of the opportunity, and really rather insulting to be called to a meeting to hear announcements that could equally well, indeed better, be typed.

This leaves the formal regular meeting, which I described earlier, free from administration (except probably for the pre-term meeting at the start of the year) and available for its central purpose: educational discussion. This cannot be overstressed; otherwise teachers will be bored, attendance will be grudging, administrative details will proliferate, and pointless discussion (i.e. over matters that no one really cares about) will expand to fill the time available. Even worse, the essential central need will be left unmet and an opportunity lost. It was good to read in the American survey I quoted earlier (page 9) that the observers did not find these faults in the departments they visited:

Department meetings are less likely to be devoted to routine administrative matters than in America. The assignment of books, collection of tests, and similar problems are handled by the department chairman in informal relations with teachers. Changes in the syllabus are a frequent topic for discussion; frequently teachers seem to discuss new ideas and methods:

film study, extensive reading, general studies, marking O level examinations, and classroom drama are typical problems of interest. Observers reported that where regular department meetings are scheduled, the department chairman usually attempts to use them for continuing education rather than for routine administrative problems – very much in contrast with practice in many American schools.[1]

Such meetings need care: advance notice of dates, well-chosen topics (not too wide), proper agendas, and a known and agreed 'guillotine' time. Various members of the department (often the 'Advisers' mentioned in the previous chapter) can be asked to give a brief introduction to the topic, and on occasions teachers can be asked to contribute a summary of a course or recent pamphlet that is relevant. Every now and again a visitor can be invited to make a specific contribution, and share experiences. He or she could be from a local school, a member of the inspectorate or advisory service, or a professional worker in some related discipline, such as a librarian, university teacher, social worker, or journalist. The discussions at well-prepared meetings should be 'too good to miss'.

The work of those meetings will relate naturally to curriculum development in Teachers' Centres, LEA courses, and even national projects. The large school department will find itself developing as virtually a teacher's centre in itself (as a few have been officially thus designated and supported), but valuable as are the internal strengths of such a large team, the Head of Department must make sure that connections are made with in-service training and development work elsewhere.

A climate of discussion can be *created*, and it must be for the ultimate formulation of broader school policy (e.g. towards examinations, reports, streaming), for the vigour of the department's subject thinking, and for the best use of the individual teacher – the subject of my next chapter.

[1] U.S. Department of Health, op. cit., p. 100.

4

Individual Needs

But, of course, it is not enough to have the right specifications, delegate responsibilities ingeniously, and create a climate of discussion. The team of teachers must be also seen as individuals, each one differing in age, background, experience, ambitions, interests, involvement, and ability, and each one requiring individual thought so that his or her contribution to the school is at its highest, as is the satisfaction of the job to the individual. That this is a two-way responsibility must be faced by the Head of Department: he needs to think of the school *and* the individual teacher, and the good of one will not be fostered without considering the good of the other. Many personal and temperamental difficulties, which in the smaller school would probably have been dealt with by the Head Teacher, will be worked out at departmental level in the larger school: whatever general arrangements the school may have for dealing with 'staff welfare' by the Deputy Head or Senior Master or Mistress, the onus of care for the individual teacher rests clearly and heavily on the care, concern, and involvement of the various Heads of Departments.

The Induction of New Teachers

Writing about staff appointments in Chapter 2, I elaborated on the need, as I see it, for fuller communication than the standard application form/short-list/formal interview. The continuation of that communication is my theme for the first stage of the Head of Department's care of the newly appointed teacher. Between the appointment and the first day of term is a vitally important time, even for experienced teachers – but is the process of induction normally managed well by schools? The general consensus seems to be that as often as not it is barely attempted. Many teachers don't even receive their timetables until the start of the new term, and join the school with only the vaguest ideas of which classes and what aspects of the subjects they will be teaching.

The following seem to me the basic requirements of common sense and common politeness: a personal letter to the successful applicant a few days after the interview (when he's often feeling a little low, wondering what it was he was so tensed up about) expressing pleasure at the appointment, indicating when he will be sent further details of the forthcoming work, and inquiring whether there are any immediate queries (accommodation, dates of term, special subject areas that need considering) that he would like answered. The timing of the next step will depend on the stage in the year: a meeting should be arranged – not necessarily in school hours – when the Head of Department can hand over a syllabus or scheme of work, any school documentation, copies of a few 'textbooks' held by the department, and so on. This is an opportunity to describe features of a department, especially those which a newcomer must know but shouldn't have to worry about when he is plunging into the first days of teaching. This may be too the time to describe the classes which he will be taking over, explaining the school's nomenclature, the composition of his particular classes, what they have been working on, and preferably (or at a later stage) making the class records available. The Head of Department will make sure that the newcomer has his address for the next holidays so that he can contact him with any queries, and will arrange a final meeting in school a day or so before term. This is a time when rooms, lockers, notice-boards, and actual classrooms can be shown, and the detailed period-by-period timetable gone over. The aim is simple (but how often fully met?): that by the time the pupils arrive the new teacher is fully conversant with the framework within which his personal teaching can flourish.

Of course, the first teaching day is not the end of the induction process: a first-year teacher commonly takes from a school more than he can give in the first year, and even an experienced teacher often finds it difficult to take in all the procedures. The Head of

Department can't remove all the difficulties, but he must be fully aware of them, and spot the need for further information or explanation before difficulties arise. This work will shade imperceptibly into the more difficult task of helping the teacher with his classes. Here the two important factors I mentioned in a more general context earlier are the basic keys: the informal togetherness and casual interflow of information, and secondly the well-established expectation of visiting classes. The new teacher is a member of a team: it must be clear that that team will support him with ideas (as discussed in the last chapter), disciplinary help (as discussed in the next chapter), and advice on small points of classroom handling and individual pupils. It is often a good idea to ask an experienced member of the department, but one younger and less 'senior' than the actual Head of Department to give an eye to a particular newcomer, for he may well speak of his difficulties more freely and, which is most important, *earlier* than he would to the Head of Department. Difficulties concerned with suitable teaching material should be met with frequent specific suggestions, those concerned with method or procedure (not that those categories are separate) by an invitation to watch the lessons of others, and the inevitable problems of 'class management' by a variety of strategies including removing individuals from classes, rearranging the timetable, visits to the class – whatever is most likely not merely to solve today's crises, but to contribute to the long-term improvement.

Deployment of Teachers
In Chapter 2 I spoke of the exploiting of individual teacher's special interests for the general advisory good of the department. What, though, of their individual timetables? How should a teacher's range of classes be planned in a comprehensive school? Even though each school and teacher has special characteristics, are there any general principles? I am taking for granted the idea that the Head of Department will have the strongest say in who teaches which class – subject only to the alteration when the total teacher team working in all subjects with a class obviously needs adjustment. There's no denying the fact that the teaching profession still has the last remnants of a prestige tradition whereby seniority and experience are rewarded by the older and more able classes, and the newcomer is given the difficult ones. Whatever

the pros and cons of the debate on the streaming of pupils, there are serious disadvantages in the streaming of teachers![1] One married woman, returning to teaching after some experience in only selective schools and then a number of years away while her children were young, was greeted as a first-year's stint with four of the least able streams in a comprehensive school; and this tale could be capped by many first-year teachers asked to take the rejects and failures of the educational system.

The proper principle is surely clear: with a few exceptions for special reasons, the comprehensive system requires teachers to work with as fair a cross-section of age and ability as possible. This is not for doctinaire theoretical reasons, but for practical educational reasons that most long-established comprehensive schools have found out for themselves. In the first place, as my own son put it from his personal experience, 'Why should the less clever classes have the worst teachers?' – and there's no doubt that they do in some schools. All groups obviously need equally skilful attention, and certainly the morale of less able groups falls drastically if they sense – as they easily do – that their teachers are the newer, younger, less well regarded of the school's staff. In the second place I am convinced that the teacher learns from a range of teaching groups, and his handling, for instance, of the more able groups is the better for his experience of the less able. The peculiar non-comprehension and almost despairing blankness that so many grammar-school teachers have with *their* 'bottom streams' is the result of limited teaching experience. Even sixth-form advanced work gains from experience teaching, say, less able fourth-year groups. Thirdly, there is the teachers' own morale. A teacher's whole work suffers if he feels the Head of Department is keeping him away from favoured classes. Lastly, only by a pattern of broadly equal sharing can the load of 'difficult' classes be kept reasonable for any one teacher. There is no doubt that an individual can bring greater resources of ideas, patience, energy, and humour to one difficult class than to many – and, incidentally, this in no way detracts from his abler classes, who, on the contrary, are also taught with greater relish for their all-the-better-appreciated qualities.

[1] Cf. the implications, even though the examples are drawn from the Primary sphere, of Brian Jackson's *Streaming: An Education System in Miniature*, Routledge and Kegan Paul, 1964.

The Head of Department's own timetable needs mentioning here: I have already made it plain that I am strongly against the tradition that gives him a major slice of the sixth-form work. In a department having difficulty recruiting fully qualified staff for national or local reasons, he may have to undertake more sixth-form work than is ideal, but this is dangerous. As I have stressed, his primary task is leading a team of teachers. He must be reconciled to the fact, indeed relish it for its implications, that his influence is wider than the pupils he teaches. Looked at like this it is obvious that his personal teaching is on the one hand symbolic – there for the example it sets – and on the other hand is for his own 'education', for what he can sample – for without this he cannot advise others or even understand their problems. The teaching load will vary, and it will always be too heavy for the comfortable carrying out of his duties,[1] but broadly I should say the head of a 'large' department (say twelve full-time teachers) should have rather more than twice the normal number of non-teaching periods. Within the teaching timetable left, it should be possible for the Head of Department to work in a reasonable cross-section of age and ability groups.

The starting-point each year is to put on to a clear chart of all the next year's classes a pencilled indication of which classes could remain with the same teacher to provide continuity. Some teachers will be leaving, and there will very likely be classes who should have a change of teacher either to give the class a contrasting personality and rather different approach, or to allow a teacher to get away from a class with which he has been having apparently unresolvable difficulties. At this point each teacher should be seen individually and his opinions sought on which classes he would like the following year. 'Your fifth-year will be gone, how about picking up a fourth-year instead?' 'You've had that less able class for two years and done a great deal with them, how about their having someone else and you taking a more clever young class?' It is usually possible to match the teachers' wishes with the Head of Department's overview, and to keep the principle of balanced timetables. But the deploying of teachers

[1] Cf. 'The heavy loads of British teachers appalled most American visitors.' (U.S. Department of Health, op. cit., page 103.) 'The English and Welsh chairmen (Heads of Departments) receive an average of only 7·8 free periods during the 40 period teaching week to attend to departmental responsibilities; Scottish chairmen receive only 9·85.' (ibid, p. 96.)

over the classes to be taught is essentially a collaborative process of personal discussion.

In fitting the department's suggestions into the central school timetable there will inevitably be difficulties. This process is done by different methods in various schools, but I should judge the effectiveness of a school's method by how well it allows the judgement of the individual Head of Department of who should teach whom to be retained (except when strong educational considerations are put forward on more general grounds). The convenience of the timetable is a bad reason for making changes, though the intricacies of a large school timetable must demand a few compromises. Some methods, though, have the wrong starting-point: for instance, to do a central period-by-period timetable *first* according to classes only, and then ask the departments to allocate teachers, makes it almost impossible for the right teacher to work with the right class: e.g. if the Head of Department feels that Mr X should teach classes A and B, but they have been timetabled to clash for three out of their five periods, he must abandon his judgement to convenience. Similarly the need in most subjects for the same teacher to have all the periods with a class should not if at all possible be sacrificed to the problems of central timetable manipulation – though sometimes it will, and then virtue should be made of a necessity by chopping off a reasonable unit (perhaps two rather than one period) and choosing the second teacher with care. If the class can't have continuity, let it have a sensible partnership.

The Teacher and the School

The individual teacher will find his role satisfaction largely within the departmental context – but not, of course, exclusively, for he is likely to have a specific pastoral role according to whatever pastoral system has been organized.[1] These two responsibilities are likely to produce tensions – ones largely unknown in the smaller selective schools. The Head of Department must resist the temptation of encouraging his teachers to skimp the pastoral assignments – arriving late for year or house groups because the search for a good worksheet is so absorbing.

But even though the main satisfaction is within the department,

[1] For a discussion of the two main systems, year or house, see *Comprehensive Schooling*, Margaret Miles, Longman, 1968, section 5, and *Pastoral Care* in this series.

and departmental recognition is a reward to the individual, the Head of Department must be aware of the need for wider recognition – he must make sure that the achievements (and, with care, the difficulties) of the individual teachers are passed on to the Head Teacher. A large school doesn't work by virtue of the Head knowing everything, and he cannot be in touch with individual teachers the whole time. However, he needs to know the key things, and the teacher needs his recognition from time to time. It may be the success he's having with a particular class, the variety and vigour of an out-of-school activity, a well devised wall display, or particularly well written reports. The Head of Department's link role is most important for the individual's feeling of being known and valued. The final stage in this work, of course, is the preparation of the notes the Head Teacher will no doubt ask for when the teacher requires a testimonial or reference when he is applying for a change of job. The Head of Department should feel that in this respect *he* has failed if many of the excellencies he finds to note at this stage are surprises to the Head Teacher.

Speaking for the Department

The last point I wish to make in this chapter is a subtle one in some ways. Any department is going to have views about wider aspects of school planning, such points as scheduling, discipline, use of rooms, and so on, which have been considered in the special context of the subject. A team of historians, for instance, is likely to have a very different point of view about school examinations from the mathematicians. Secondly, each department is likely to devise various schemes that impinge in a practical way on the school organization: a visit out of school, a full-length film, a team-teaching sequence. These schemes need putting across to the rest of the staff, and their practical arrangements carefully integrating. Thirdly, departmental views are going to be canvassed by the Head Teacher towards decisions he is formulating. In all these three respects the members of the department must feel confident that their Head of Department speaks for them with fidelity and force. This point cannot be exaggerated: unless the teachers feel that the voice of the department gathers the individual views fully, synthesises them carefully, and puts them across vigorously there will be a series of practical difficulties, confusions, and clashes, and, perhaps worse, a growing malaise and disintegration which is painful to see and worse to experience.

The satisfaction of the individual teacher in the large school, it can be truly said, depends on the pivotal role of the Head of Department. He must spare no effort in ensuring the welfare of each member of his team, for it is the sum of each of those that creates the overall health of the school.

5

The Pupils Themselves

The Head of Department's ultimate responsibilities, of course, are to the pupils of the school. If they have had scant mention in the previous four chapters of this book it is because the Head of Department's method of fulfilling that responsibility is primarily by leading his team of teachers. To hope to help, say, 1,500 pupils by direct contact or action is clearly a delusion. Indeed to have a significant *personal* effect on the subject learning of many more than those pupils for whom he is personally responsible as class teacher is impossible. There are a few exceptions to this generalization, and I shall touch on them in this chapter, but it is essential to see this clearly. The rather more 'personal' teaching subjects, in which I should include most of the humanities, are undoubtedly tempting in this way. The point is analogous to that which faces a Head Teacher: he has to a major extent lost the opportunity to work directly with pupils, and the few special cases in which he intervenes personally in no way contradict this broad principle. Indeed in the large school the Head Teacher has to see himself working almost exclusively through his senior colleagues – and not often directly with individual teachers. These are not the kind of points much discussed in educational literature, though they are vital. One interesting case study is the much publicized Risinghill school difficulties. The debate has tended to churn over whether the Headmaster's *ideals* were right: what comes out of the very sympathetic book on the school's brief history[1] is that the Headmaster, Michael Duane, was endeavouring to work (whether from

[1] *Risinghill, Death of a Comprehensive School*, Leila Berg, Penguin Books, 1968, e.g. p. 221–2.

force of circumstances or because of his own attitudes is difficult to judge) too often *directly* with pupils, and was not struggling sufficiently to exert his influence by building up teacher teams. In other words, if it were fair to apportion any blame to him, the blame would not concern his educational ideas but his management strategies.

However, all this is not to say that the Head of Department's personal dealings with pupils are unimportant: far from it. How he speaks to a pupil, follows up a tardy piece of homework, writes a report, keeps a House Head or Year Teacher informed are all extremely important, not merely for the pupils concerned but as influences on the rest of the departmental team. There is no doubt at all that brusque, casual, or uninterested attention to individual pupils by a Head of Department is reflected many times over throughout a department.

But the possibilities of individual care must be institutionalized, and cannot merely be left to personal influence. Given, though, the combination of personal example and properly devised procedures, the larger school is capable, I maintain, of giving greater individual care to pupils than the smaller. This comes from two points, ones which detractors of the large school often cite as objections.

Firstly, though every pupil is known very well indeed to the relevant number of teachers (as many as in any other school, however small), they are *not* known to all the teachers. The effects of this are misunderstood. They can be demonstrated when adult and pupil meet at a swing door somewhere in a school corridor. Here the reality of school relationships are revealed. In the smaller school, certainly if the pupil is past his first year, adult and young person at once recognize and know each other – or more likely because they would recognize each other if they troubled to they simply take each other for granted. In the larger school such a meeting is a genuine confrontation. If the two do know each other from past teaching the greeting is likely to be genuine – that is the picking up of a past relationship, for the flicker of memory has not been blunted by innumerable meetings throughout the week. Equally likely, though, is that the pupil does not know who this adult is. In the large school strangers are not stared at or giggled over. The pupil at the swing door may not recognize the adult at all. To him the adult may be visitor, electrician, teacher, or parent.

How the two get through the door is real, and not conditioned by the over familiarity of too close a knowledge.

This lack of inevitable personal knowledge can be exploited by using a second person, usually the Head of Department, to see a pupil and his work. The Head of Department uses the time and energy of the tutor or form-master in their pastoral care not for continuous attention to a limited group of pupils, but for short bursts of intensive attention to those pupils referred to him for a variety of reasons. The referals may be 'disciplinary' in a fairly narrow sense, or they may be for a second opinion on a certain aspect of the pupil's work (his mathematical background giving him difficulty in Physics, curiously backward spelling in English, or failures of understanding in aspects of History). From time to time, though, the individual teacher will suggest that a pupil sees the Head of Department for advice. This is particularly interesting with older pupils who may wish to follow up some special branch of the subject, know of related activities elsewhere, discuss further education establishments, or simply talk about books or visits.

The second point is that size and numbers of staff make it possible to sort matters out, devise proper procedures that can be continued, and organize the subsidiary paperwork. Two institutions are especially valuable in my experience: well kept departmental record cards for each pupil, and a daily 'surgery' or interview session after school each day.

Undoubtedly the larger school creates paperwork: to refuse to accept this is to produce muddle and, paradoxically, to waste rather than save time. The school will have a central record system – it will no doubt bring together Primary School records, secondary school report copies, correspondence with parents, and records of any significant interviews with staff. However, each department is likely to feel the need of a record that is more specific to its own subject requirements, and which is close to the hand of the Head of Department. It might be possible in smaller comprehensive schools to combine this with the main filing system where the layout of the school does not make this too cumbersome. Generally, though, it will be found more convenient and more effective to maintain departmental records by the Head of Department's desk. Each subject will have a different kind of need: some may be able to sum up the pupil's progress and attitude adequately in a brief letter or number notation (which if possible should have a comparable validity across departments). They may be able to maintain a single sheet for a class or set unit, and follow a pupil from one to the other as he changes class. Other departments will have a small index card for each pupil, suitably ruled, which will give space not only for a grading notation, but also for the occasional footnote if there is special need for it. For an English department, with its close personal involvement with pupils, and the many facets to its work, I have found something larger is required; the size I have found most useful was 8 in. × 13 in., and the details were printed on a thin but not too flexible card. Starting with the key information copied from the Junior School record (called a 'Primary Profile' in the ILEA), it included twice-yearly grades, and once a year as full a description as possible by the class English teacher. The right-hand column was kept for notes on any correspondence, interviews, or special central matters concerning the pupil.[1] Such record cards are invaluable when taking over a new teaching group or receiving a single pupil whose class has been changed. They can be consulted by the Head of Department whenever a pupil is referred to him, a parent writes in, or another member of staff makes a specific inquiry. As a cumulative record they are essential to provide continuity in these days of fairly rapid staff turnover, and greatly assist the detailed care which the department can offer the pupils.

One of the most frequent uses for these record cards in a large department is, I suggest, for the daily 'surgery'. I have already indicated the need for a senior member of the department being willing to help with guiding on disciplining pupils – even if only as a fresh adult. It is also implicit in the team concept that I described in Chapter 2 that the resources of the department as a whole should be available to offer mutual support for discipline and diagnosis. Some Heads of Departments can be available only occasionally, and therefore only for sporadic and single sessions with pupils; the Heads of large departments, though, should be able to be more frequently, and in a school of over 1,500 will probably need to be. A simple reporting system, with the familiar daily blank initialled by the class teacher with a grade to indicate whether the pupil's attitude and application have been satisfactory,

[1] Teachers interested in the devising of suitable record cards may like to consult the elaborate and detailed card for Physical Education devised by Leslie Keating, and included in his book *The School Report*, Kenneth Mason, 1969, p. 41. See also Chapter 10 of *Pastoral Care* (in this series).

is presented to the Head of Department who, with record card to hand, can inspect the pupil's work, talk over the situation, and specify a reporting period. 'What sanctions?' may well be asked. That is a separate discussion, and one for the individual school, but my point here is that such a continous, personal, and reliable support service for the teachers in the team makes talk of sanctions largely irrelevant: it is the care and involvement, if necessary the seeing of parents, that more often than not saves the pupil from worse behaviour.

Each school, again, will have its own division between the pastoral organization and the academics. It is essential, of course, that the pastoral organization is fed by the department with detailed information by the subject teacher. If the Head of Department has to see a pupil, the 'tutor' must be told. I do not see any conflict, as is often feared by teachers hearing of this kind of pupil guidance for the first time, between the pastoral and the academic staff, provided that the Head of Department is rigorous in meeting this need for full information. If the pupil is in trouble all round, then the Head of House or Year Master will need to deal with the matter; if it seems, for the moment at least, confined to a particular subject, then that Head of Department is the person.

However, this raises a wider point about the pastoral care of pupils – a matter which has not had adequate airing and discussion as a necessary corollary to comprehensive reorganization. I have used frequently the metaphor of 'pastoral' because there are a variety of organizational patterns, and within each there is considerable variation in the degree of responsibility delegated 'down' the pastoral channels – in one school the Year Teacher will retain the traditional 'Head Teacher' activities of, for instance, letters to parents, seeing pupils when they are in minor trouble. However, the metaphor in 'pastoral' is not ideal. The shepherd/flock relationship is not a fully appropriate analogy for the care that a school takes with a pupil. In particular it suggests a kind of abstracted care without activity. This is seen at its worst in schools where a 'Senior Master' or 'Senior Mistress' figure has too large a share of disciplinary functions passed upwards. Disciplining in a vacuum is less effective than when it is kept in a specific working context. Similarly pastoral care works only in certain (valuable, though) ways when it is severed from the subject teaching context which is the predominant working context for the pupil. To be specific: if a second-year pupil has exasperated a new young teacher, should the pupil be dealt with by, say, his Head of House or the Head of Department? Of course there is no universal answer, and it will depend on a multitude of factors, but it is worth being clear what each has to offer: the Head of House will probably have a greater knowledge of the pupil and his past. There is, too, a disadvantage: the session may degenerate into a vague repetition of: 'Well, what is it this time? Didn't I tell you the last time . . . ?' The Head of Department, on the other hand, has a greater knowledge of the teaching context in which the misbehaviour took place. He has the material of the subject in common with the pupil, something that can be used as a valuable medium for the discussion and, it must be stressed, allows a closer analysis of what exactly the pupil did that displeased, and what might have led to it. There is, too, a disadvantage here: the Head of Department will probably have insufficient time to establish a real relationship. But even this can be turned to good effect, and I am convinced that newly reorganized schools should not allow the apparent simplicity and clarity of a carefully devised pastoral/academic structure, important as it is to have such a structure well defined, to create too sharp a division of labour. The department has an inevitable and right concern for the progress that every pupil makes in that subject area: learning or behaviour difficulties that reveal themselves in that particular subject context are often best resolved by the Head of Department himself, and not simply passed across to the pastoral side. The Head of Department, it needs remembering, has the overwhelming advantage of being able to say, 'Well, if *that* bored you, how was it you wrote a good story last month?' or 'It's not true that your teacher only does exercises; last week your class did this or that'. Some part of the pastoral care of the school is best left in departmental hands, working closely with the other part of the organization that maintains the total care of the pupil. And furthermore it will be found that only in this way can the Head of Department support his teachers fully.

6

The Subject

To leave the subject taught to sixth place may seem to some to indicate that the sense of priorities has been lost, and the cynic will add that such relegation is typical of the compromises forced on teachers by the large comprehensive school. Of course, as my book is not about the teaching of any subject, but hopes to help the Head of Department lead an organization through which any subject can effectively be taught, there is no real place for a discussion of subject teaching: to have embarked on that would have limited me to my own specialist field, English, but, more than that, it would have changed the nature of my book. I want to look at what is organizationally significant to departments, and thus to the reality of subject teaching, and most of what I have to say is, I am convinced, relevant across the departments.

However, there is in any case a further reason for this seeming relegation. Well thought out theories of subject approach may be fundamental, but the Head of Department must relate them to his ability to lead his team, and his understanding and knowledge of the pupils. Some compromise is probably inevitable: partly because the one person's view of the subject is likely to be inadequate and to benefit by drawing into it the views of others, but also because an approach that can't be put into practice by *this* team is wrong for *this* team. It may well be that there will be a gradual change in the personnel, outlook, and competence of the team, but at all times the theory must match the possible, preferably just leading it and spurring it on.

In this chapter I should like to suggest some points about the translation of subject teaching ideas into departmental practice which touch most subjects. These, then, are aspects which I feel any Head of Department should consider. In most cases all I have provided are memo headings, jottings to serve as a check list for the subject specialist who is anxious to put his subject ideas into a comprehensive school.

(i) *Specialist versus General*

It would not be an unfair caricature of the grammar-school aims and approaches, I think, to say that the purpose of most of the work is to produce the university entrant: three forms of first-years are the base of a pyramid which will produce a peak of x number of university specialists. I am not saying that no care is taken of the rest who progressively reveal themselves as unsuitable for the peak. However, it is usually presumed that the specialist diet, or what each can digest of it, is correct for all. The comprehensive school Head of Department must have a different perspective: he too must make sure that the necessary foundations are laid for any pupil who may later wish to be a specialist linguist. But, more than that, the Head of Department must ask what his subject has to offer the general student, the ordinary adult. This contrast produces a real conflict in some subjects. Take music, for instance: the study of music has always been a very specialist activity, indeed even musicians have generation after generation revolted against the narrow academicism that seems to get locked into their education. A potential performer needs early and intensive technical training. What is needed, though, by the majority? The intake of a grammar school normally receive a standard syllabus which is the first layer of the O-level course. But how many will take O-level? How many ought to, even? Is *this* the appropriate education for the ordinary person? Is there not a need for looking at a 'general' education in listening which will relate to the specialist needs, but stand on its own also?[1] Classics, which would seem the most difficult area in which to resolve this conflict, has been revolutionized by the Schools Council/Nuffield Cambridge Non-Linguistic Classics Project. This, it seems to me, has a significance far beyond that particular subject because what

[1] For an excellent discussion of the general versus specialist theme in the field of music see *Sound and Silence*, John Paynter and Peter Aston, C.U.P. 1970. There are valuable ideas in the study of society, but which have a wide general application, in *Men and Society*, Ed. Robert Irvine-Smith, Heinemann Educational Books, 1968.

has been produced is a *philosophy* of general education in the secondary school.[1] Every Head of Department must lead his team towards resolving the possibly conflicting demands, but faced with an intake of, say, 300 pupils careful thought about the contribution of the subject to a real 'general' education is needed.

(ii) *A Common Core*

In a middle school, junior high school, or in the first three years of an all-through comprehensive school, whether it is fully or only partially streamed, the acute problem has to be faced that if the comprehensive system is to be true to its ideals the possibilities of flexibility must remain open. A comprehensive school is not a multilateral school[2] – and it is up to each department to consider how the subject can be taught to maintain flexibility of movement and a range of decisions for the pupil later in his school life. (This problem is related to that of (i) above.) The years between eleven and fourteen must allow for separate and individual growth, but must not contain curricula elements that will band pupils irrevocably. It is already clear that comprehensive schools are only partially successful in giving a greater range of opportunities, and streamed schools offer only a limited chance of regrouping.[3] Most schools, or groups of schools, will see the fourteen-to-sixteen period as the one for differentiation by interest, career, and specific (as opposed to general) abilities. In 'factual' (e.g. Geography) and closely structured subjects (e.g. Mathematics) very great care is needed in devising this 'common core' syllabus of the foundation years.[4]

(iii) *The Remedial*

There are a variety of arguments for and against the separation of the band of least able children from the more able stream of the

[1] Published by the Cambridge University Press in 1970. Cf. also J. E. Sharwood Smith, Head of the Classics Department, University of London Institute of Education: *Classics Teaching: Its Nature and Contribution to Education, Bulletin*, New Series, Number 20, Spring Term, 1970.

[2] For a valuable historical description see *The Evolution of the Comprehensive School*, David Rubinstein and Brian Simon, Routledge and Kegan Paul, 1968, especially Chapter 5.

[3] Cf. *Social Class and the Comprehensive School*, Julienne Ford, Routledge and Kegan Paul, 1969, which though it has many statistical and conceptual faults demonstrates in this respect failure in one school.

[4] Cf. *Curriculum Process*, D. K. Wheeler, University of London Press, 1967, and the volume on curriculum planning in this series.

curriculum and teaching pattern. Broadly, these pupils need small groups even more urgently, fewer teachers, and a skill which is related to patience and variety. On the other hand, there is a continuum of ability, not a strong break, and the curriculum should reflect this, and the less able can be further dulled if their diet is less varied because they have fewer and less specialized teachers. It is not relevant to discuss the remedial curriculum and teaching methods here; however the new Head of Department, who is likely to have had little actual teaching experience with such pupils, should make a point, even in a school which has a strongly organized separate remedial 'department', of establishing very close links, getting some personal contact, arranging for some of his teachers to work with remedial classes, and ensuring that the books, teaching materials, and schemes of work have, at least, an awareness of each other between his department and the specifically remedial.

(iv) *Pupil Groupings*

These last considerations impinge on the difficult but central question of pupil groupings, and it is a matter about which the Head of Department should ponder both from the point of view of the total education of the growing pupil, and in particular from that of his subject specialism. His may be a school that streams by 'general' undifferentiated ability for the younger years at least; it may, to go to the other extreme, be a school where from the first year onwards he receives to be taught at certain periods in the week a gathering of, say, ninety pupils, with provision for three teaching groups, it then being his responsibility to decide upon the method of grouping.[1] Certainly he is likely to find some such blocking arrangement in the fourth and fifth years, and needs therefore, to have a policy towards setting and grouping.[2] It is obvious, of course, that there is an interaction between teaching methods and pupil grouping methods. It is all the more important that the department should have as clear an understanding as

[1] For a description of a system of this sort see A. W. Rowe's article 'I Abolished Streaming', *New Education*, April, 1967, and there is a somewhat similar approach in *Going Comprehensive*, by E. S. Conway, Harrap, 1970. There is a balanced introduction to methods of pupil grouping in an article by S. E. Gunn, 'Teaching Groups in Secondary Schools', in *Trends*, No. 19, H.M.S.O., July, 1970.

[2] The pupil record cards I described on page 42 above will be found invaluable for setting.

possible of this interaction. Some American research has shown that pupil/teacher compatibility is the most effective method of 'streaming', and I know of one secondary school where first-year general streaming was mainly on the basis of seeming maturity. Certainly I have found that in the teaching of English and I think the Humanities more generally, a teaching method that relies heavily on personal exchange of reactions and views[1] functions far better if the 'setting' is carefully based on the character and past behaviour of pupils, so that explosive groups are broken up, teacher/pupil incompatibilities avoided, and each teaching group built up by a system of balanced hand-picking like a selection for a team.

The debate of the seventies and after is going to be about the internal grouping of pupils – not so much 'selection' but rather 'segregation'. This debate must be based on careful observation and thinking at subject department level.

(v) Difficult Areas

The Head of Department will look at his subject with the whole school in mind equally, and he will relate the various aspects of work in an organic and carefully interlocking way. All the same, there are various sections of secondary education that pose special problems – or, to put it another way, pose the general problems more acutely. Two of these are 'the young school leaver' (curious euphemism that) in the fourth and fifth years, and the non-specialist in the sixth form. Again, all I wish to attempt here is to focus attention on the problems as ones which the Head of Department will at least consider before applying for his post, and will make sure his department squarely face as soon as possible.

The fairly general pattern of offering a wide variety of options and thus regrouping virtually all the pupils as they enter the fourth is one of the distinctive features which differentiates comprehensive schools from secondary modern schools. The less able pupils in the fourth year have been treated in a variety of ways. An increasing

[1] Cf. the work of the Schools Council/Nuffield *Humanities Curriculum Project*, the material and description of which have been published by Heinemann Educational Books, 1970, and which has been summed up in a number of articles by the Director, Lawrence Stenhouse, including *The Humanities Curriculum Project*, Journal of Curriculum Studies, Volume 1, Number 1, November, 1968, Wm. Collins & Co. Ltd.

number of schools have devised coherent 'Leavers' courses with unified syllabuses. This, though, is a pattern that depends on a fair degree of confidence about staying-on decisions. In areas where the level of voluntary staying on has been high, such a 'closed' grouping has been less appropriate for coping with the many different points at which pupils make up their minds whether to stay on or leave. The raising of the school leaving age in 1973 may have favoured the first of these patterns, but I doubt if any compartmentalizing of pupils will prove right in the long run. They need a variety of kinds of provision, and the large school is well placed to offer these, rather than homogeneous package deals.

However the fourth and fifth year are organized, the Head of Department will recognize that the curriculum for the less able needs especial thought – made paradoxically more difficult by the opportunities to take C.S.E. in at least a small number of subjects that are realistic for all but a tiny number of pupils. 1973 magnified the problems: for the first time a large number of young adults are in the education system with no ambitions or prospects for further education – that is without the future career reward which attention to schooling can provide their more able and amenable colleagues. Their needs require special attention. Most of the public debate has been very general, though the Schools Council Working Papers do particularize at a subject level and should be consulted fully even outside particular subject areas, for it is amazing what useful similarities can be found between such diverse subjects as, for instance, Rural Studies and History, or Technology and English when considering the shaping of the teaching pattern.[1] This is clearly a topic that can be looked at in occasional department meetings, and the whole machinery of discussion which I described in Chapter 3 needs bringing to bear on it. Further, the topic is one in which teachers' centres could combine to develop area ideas.[2]

[1] The most closely relevant Schools Council Documents to date are: *Working Papers*, Numbers 1, *Science for the Young School Leaver*, 1965; 2, *Raising the School Leaving Age*, 1965; 11, *Society and the Young School Leaver*, 1967; 14, *Mathematics for the Majority*, 1967; 15, *Counselling in Schools*, 1967; 17, *Community Service and the Curriculum*, 1968; 27, *'Cross'd with Adversity'*, 1970. Also the series *Humanities for the Young School Leaver: An Approach Through Classics*, 1967; *An Approach Through English*, 1968; *An Approach Through History*, 1969. Some valuable research findings about pupils and parents' attitudes will be found in *Enquiry 1, Young School Leavers*, 1969.

[2] I have developed a tentative sketch of possible approaches in English and the Humanities in my *Towards the New Fifth*, Longman, 1969.

The logistics of the sixth form are complicated. At a time when the examination pattern is undergoing changes it is impossible to be specific, but the essence of the problem will remain: how to provide sufficient teaching levels and directions for the range of pupils staying on into the sixth, as far as possible avoiding the pattern or mere repetition of failed earlier courses.

(vi) *Inter-Disciplinary Work*

The subject specialisms have come under extensive criticism because of the artificial and isolated teaching they can produce. Many schools have produced schemes for integrated studies which suffer from insufficient planning or resources, and despite considerable success at all levels,[1] especially the first and the fourth years, the basic questions remain, how should subject specialists work together, and how can specialisms illuminate each other? As I have already implied in the first four chapters, a large comprehensive school builds up strong self-contained departments. A further responsibility of each of their Heads is to ensure that the points of contact are kept sensitive and active.

(vii) *The Scheme of Work*

Syllabuses and Schemes of Work have a bad reputation – there to play safe with inspectors but not for any real purpose. There is also what seems an illogical but common notion that a Scheme of Work must of its nature be *cramping* to the individual teacher. For such reasons the written statement of the Head of Department is often little valued and little used. I have no sympathy with these objections to a department having a proper Scheme of Work (though I don't like that title much). If it suffers from the faults hinted at above, then it is a bad Scheme of Work, and the existence of a bad Scheme of Work does not mean there can be no good ones. To say, as one inspector did, that 'All that really matters about a music teaching syllabus can be written on the back of a cigarette packet' may well be true – but is all the more reason for expanding such basic truths with suggestions, examples, recommendations exemplifying such pithy wisdom. To say that a teacher needs room to manœuvre is, again, not an objection to the existence of a scheme.

---

[1] See, for instance, the issue of the University of London *Bulletin* for Autumn, 1969, New Series No. 19 (available free from the Institute, at Malet Street, W.C.1).

A proper scheme of work is an essential tool for the complementary team concept I discussed earlier; it is doubly important in the large comprehensive school when the unity has to incorporate a large number of teachers. The teacher, however new or inexperienced, should be helped by the syllabus to know where he is going, to be given all the helpful suggestions possible, but to be left with the purposeful freedom that can come only within a recognized framework. It is a document that sums up and maintains the common purpose of experienced specialist, newcomer, non-specialist, untrained graduate, part-timer, student, and auxiliary staff (e.g. librarian, audio-visual aids worker, laboratory and studio assistant). It provides a way of picturing for other departments, the Head Teacher, Inspectorate, and teacher-training institutions with which the school works the aims and techniques of the department. It will never, of course, be a final document, and is best designed on a loose-leaf system with separate sections that can be revised and reinserted as the ideas of the department evolve. Then sections will often be the result of general discussion, drafted by the relevantly interested 'Adviser' or another member of the department.

What might it contain? Perhaps I could illustrate the various aspects mainly from the point of view of an English department – a subject in which there is very little 'content' and in which, therefore, the need for a Scheme of Work is often derided.[1] My headings are not offered as sections of an actual scheme, nor would the resulting fully worked out scheme necessarily be written up in this order:

(a) A descriptive sketch of the meaning of 'English' for this school – i.e. an attempt to summarize the philosophy of the subject teaching which the department shares, and which, though not immutable, informs all that follows.

(b) Possible ways of organizing the work, i.e. of providing continuity. This is a need in many subjects (e.g. Music) which do not have a strongly felt pedagogic structure, as well as many which are breaking out of past structures (e.g. in History, where chronology is becoming far less dominant).[2]

[1] Cf. The English Department Syllabus, Norman Hidden, in the University of London Bulletin, New Series Number 17, Spring Term 1969.

[2] I have sketched possible ways of organizing work in English in my contribution, 'Mainstream', to the symposium on the teaching of English, Directions, edited by Deys Thompson, Cambridge University Press, 1969.

(c) A clear list, with explanations where it might be necessary, of any specific points, facts, or techniques which the department have agreed shall be taught. If there is an agreed timing for these points it will be clearly noted. However large or small this agreed list, it must be adhered to.

(d) An extensive list of suggestions, hints, ideas for lesson patterns, and activities, and ways of putting things across. Such a list is indispensable for the teacher in his first two years, and will be found surprisingly useful by the experienced teacher whose memory is jogged by flicking over the pages.

(e) Recommended Reading: all subjects should have their lists of books for pupils: There are not many books that a first- or second-year pupil can read in connection with Mathematics, for instance, but those that can be recommended should be listed in the syllabus, and duplicated copies of the list kept. For subjects such as History such lists are obviously of great importance.

To the teacher of English the lists – by age, and type of book – are essential tools. Gleaned from the suggestions of the team and cross checked by discussion and the swopping of titles that goes on in a large group of English teachers, the lists save the individual teacher time and widen his scope.

(f) Administrative Points: Every subject has its administrative problems – coping with timber and tools, books and paper, or chemicals and apparatus – and its agreed procedures for home-work and so forth. Once settled, these should be clearly listed for the scheme of work. It may look bureaucratic, but its result is the opposite. There is no freedom in muddle, and many Heads of Departments inherit depressing muddle.

A scheme of work with components such as these will take some time to build up; indeed the replacement of some sections may have started before its planned outline is complete. The newly appointed Head of Department will normally be wise to wait a while before undertaking the revision of whatever he finds – indeed he may find a considerable section that can stand. (Though this is unlikely, as a departing Head of Department normally thinks it wiser to leave the Scheme of Work alone in his final year or so.) He should not, I suggest, be deceived by notions of pseudo 'freedom' to think that a Scheme of Work is a strait-jacket to be struggled out of. It is an essential formulation of the subject policy which it is the responsibility of a Head of Department to lead his department towards establishing.

7

Facilities

The truth that good teaching grows out of good relationships with pupils, and that 'personality' is therefore of major importance, has been allowed to disguise an almost equal truth: that physical provision, equipment, and teaching 'materials' almost literally control the method and style of the teaching. All the efforts that I have described in the previous chapters will be hampered, if not severely warped, if the facilities for the departmental team are inadequate. Improvization and ingenuity are virtues no doubt, but the object of school administration is not to foster them above all else, and, anyway, even improvization and ingenuity need raw materials to work on. The Head of Department owes it to his teachers to provide suitable facilities as fully and effectively as possible, both because it is an elementary duty of leadership to provide the wherewithall, but even more significantly because in all aspects of the secondary school, what happens between teacher and taught is affected as much, if not more, by materials and physical provision as by ideas in the abstract. A History teacher provided with a class set of 'comprehensive' textbooks for the year is forced to provide a different texture of lessons from one given access to catalogued stocks of worksheets; a Music teacher obliged to negotiate for a record player and to carry it up flights of stairs to his room will use records less than one with equipment permanently set up in the classroom – and this will markedly effect the meaning of 'music' for the pupil; a Science class taking place in a tiered 'lecture theatre' with one 'demonstration' bench will have an entirely different experience from its peers in a laboratory –

and the difference will affect the pupils' notion of what 'science' is about.

Approaches

It may seem strange that I should have said, 'it is an elementary duty of leadership to *provide*', for surely, many would ask, it is the duty of LEA administrators to 'provide'? Too often, though, departments are thwarted not because of LEA parsimoniousness or even lack of will, but because the Head of Department has been satisfied to sit and wait, or has merely moaned at the wrong time and to the wrong person. It is very noticeable that successful departments have by and large a fair and growing proportion of what they want, whilst unsuccessful departments languish, apparently unfairly, without. This is because one of the key factors in a successful department is its ability to articulate clearly its broad teaching aims, translate these into clear procedures, and thus be able to specify with some precision what is required in the way of accommodation, equipment, and teaching materials to make these aims operational. This descriptive task comes first, and requires a clear understanding of the teaching aims supported by a comparison with teaching facilities elsewhere and with any reference material that may have been produced. No one would effectively argue the case for improved music or drama space in a particular school without studying the *Building Bulletin* devoted to these two types of work, or consider the problems of sixth-form accommodation without studying the proposals and specifications in the two relevant *Bulletins*.[1] Such reading would be supplemented by visits to other schools, possibly information from the specialist subject associations, and consultations with the LEA Advisers or Inspectors. A member of the department can collate all the team's ideas and this range of external information and produce a convincing summary. Obviously idealism will have to be tempered with reality, but the aim should be to describe what should be done.

However, to define is not to obtain, and the Head of Department needs to know how to press the department's claims. The channels will vary from authority to authority and school to

[1] *Drama and Music*, Building Bulletin No. 30, H.M.S.O., 1966; *Sixth Form and Staff* Building Bulletin No. 25, H.M.S.O., 1965; *Sixth Form Centre*, Building Bulletin No 41, H.M.S.O., 1967.

school, and an early priority for a new Head of Department is to map the channels, as it were. This will include the internal procedures of the school (It is particularly difficult for teachers coming from small schools to appreciate the delegated powers held by senior staff other than the Head Teacher), the powers of the governors, and the LEA's ordering and financial provision. It is often far from simple to discover precisely to whom a request for, say, a loop projector should be addressed. Must it be requisitioned and paid for from the annual departmental capitation allowance? Does the school have central funds for equipment from which such an item can be bought? Or would it be available from the LEA as basic provision at no charge to the school if the request is made to the right section in the right way? Many authorities have excellent central facilities for the supply or loan of equipment, but it is more rare for this availability to be clearly documented. It almost never happens that a new Head of Department is given a chart or document which states all the sources of facilities. (We still suffer from the tradition of the Headmaster who supposedly knows all and does everything; this figure handles the annual requisition, and those working in this mould still like to scrutinize the details of departmental ordering. Such centralizing is hopeless in the large organization.)

When the methods and procedures have been discovered the Head of Department will put in his requests to the right person, and here I would make a tiny but essential point: forward the request with a carbon copy, and keep a third in the department's file. Some device for checking the progress of the request is essential. A large organization can have dated files which come up for consideration each day; the copy of the request is then placed into the file for, say, a month ahead. A simpler device is to make a jotting in your diary six or eight weeks ahead: 'check cupboard request'. If it hasn't been answered, a fresh one is sent. The Head of Department learns to take 'No' for an answer, but he must insist on *an* answer, and not let legitimate requests go into limbo.

Accommodation

Of course the most significant type of facility available is that over which there is least control: accommodation. However, the Head of Department will want to review the current use of the school's accommodation: Are there ways in which specialist needs could be more fully met by a rearrangement of rooms? Are his team timetabled to give them most access to specialist materials and the most continuity in their rooms? (It is tempting for a Head of Department to concern himself with his own comfort and ease, but his prime concern should be to scrutinize the rooms timetable to see if his team are best placed.) Secondly, he will want to make sure that the existing accommodation is as well fitted as it could be: cupboards, shelves, screens, possibly black-out, and furniture can often be improved, altered, or rearranged to make better use of the present rooms. Thirdly, he will want to keep himself well informed about any plans for conversions, extensions, or re-building. This is not a far-fetched point: during periods of school reorganization, the expansion of school population, and in the years following the raising of the school leaving age there are few large schools in which there is not some building programme in the offing. The right points are to be made at the right time to make the best use of these opportunities.

Equipment
Only in the sciences and in a few isolated innovations such as the Schools Council Project Technology has the defining and quanti-fying of equipment needs kept pace with curriculum thinking. In the humanities in particular curricula ambition has far overshot the resources available so that there is a serious tension. From the Newsom Report[1] onwards, and through a series of Schools Council *Working Papers*, there has been a consistent failure to work out the details of the necessary facilities,[2] yet all the recommended trends imply a radical change from textbook-based work to a range of equipment.

The larger school paradoxically both offers new possibilities of equipment, and at the same time makes its handling more difficult. Size means that minority-demand equipment can be justified and economically used: thus central sound-recording facilities or a properly equipped projection theatre should be possible for the school, and, for instance, an English department could have a loop projector, or a Commerce department an electronic stencil cutter.

[1] *Half our Future*, H.M.S.O., 1964.
[2] Working Paper No. 17, *Community Service and the Curriculum* (H.M.S.O., 1968) has a small exception, pointing out the need for additional telephone provision and clerical assistance (para. 69).

Thought is required to provide the basic equipment with the necessary accessories to make sure that it can be used to the maximum effect. An extension lead, for instance, is frequently needed if a tape-recorder is to be placed in the best position in the classroom. A proper system is required for the booking, collection, and, maintenance of the equipment. The old way of the Head of Department virtually nursing a tape-recorder as if it were his or her personal prize won't do. Maintenance is a larger problem than it sounds. There is ample evidence that much teaching time is lost and much public money wasted by being tied up in idle equipment through poor maintenance procedures. This criticism is based on personal experience, observation in many schools, hearsay, and the outsider's remarks in the U.S. survey which I quoted earlier: 'In Britain, low usage [of audio-visual aids] reflects the economic condition of most schools: aids tend to be unavailable *or in a state of disrepair*.'[1] The italics are mine, for although the first reason for low usage may be irremedial, the second is surely not.

Even in a small department, the Head of Department is not going to be able to look after the equipment himself, but he must press the Authority for an adequate maintenance service (*undoubtedly audio-visual aids technicians are required in all but the smallest secondary schools*), delegate clearly the responsibility for oversight of the department's equipment, and insist that all members of the team follow the agreed procedure.

Printed Material

For Mathematics, most of the humanities, and such important areas of the school curriculum as sixth-form General Studies, printed study material will always continue to be the central learning resource, whether in the form of sets of books, the library stock, sets of specially prepared worksheets, or packs of related but miscellaneous facsimiles.[2] In most of these subjects the old linear-organized 'course book' has literally exploded, and instead of taking our pupils through the course from chapter one to the last section, teachers in most of the humanities at least direct their pupils to a range of disparate material which is evaluated and from

[1] Squire and Applebee, op. cit., p. 77.
[2] e.g. *The Jackdaw Series* (Jonathan Cape); the *Archive Units*, of the University of Newcastle; the similar sets produced by the *University of Northern Ireland*; or my own *The Times' Authors* (published by *The Times*)

which the relevant facts are derived, attitudes deduced, and through which the experience of learning can be obtained.

I have written elsewhere of the implications of those developments for the stocking, organization, and use of the secondary school library,[1] but it is necessary to stress here that the Head of a subject department has a responsibility to ensure that the professional librarian (for I regard professional non-teaching staff here as essential, though this point obviously applies even if a teacher runs the library) is advised on the books and materials (e.g. pamphlets, Press-cutting, artefacts, printed ephemera, prints, slides, tapes, discs, etc.) required for the whole range of pupils, both for classroom work and private interest. In the grammar-school tradition the library has tended to be primarily stocked for the older pupil, and many Heads of Departments when pressed for library recommendations produce lists of definitely sixth-form books. The young mathematician and the young biologist need encouraging to read around their special interests, and the library must be appropriately stocked. Many departments curiously fail to ask the library to stock the background and other books actually recommended in the class textbooks used. Even books recommended to pupils by teachers are often not held by the library!

Within the more narrow confines of the classroom, learning departments are likely to amass and stock a great and diverse quantity of teaching material.[2] It seems certain that the future provision of the properly planned secondary school will include a central store in close association with the library (for it is illogical and growing increasingly unrealistic to draw a rigid line between 'library' resources and 'teachers' resources – they need to be centrally available through a unified catalogue). Full-time storekeepers will then deal with organizing, maintaining, issuing, checking, and ordering (to the teachers' requests).[3] Undoubtedly, however, in the near future this officially almost unrecognized burden will continue to be dispersed round the department or the school. Either way the Head of Department must clarify how

---

[1] Cf. Section 3 of Chapter 6 of *Towards the New Fifth*, Longman, 1969. The work of the Schools Council General Studies project under Robert Irvine-Smith at York University is central to the use of the library for a whole range of subjects.

[2] It is essential to have a regular system for scrutinizing all new teaching material that educational publishers produce.

[3] Cf. *An Instructional Materials Centre*, Norman W. Beswick, in *The School Librarian*, Vol. 15, No. 2, July 1967, and *Resources for Learning in a School* in this series.

materials relate to teaching aims in terms of type, storage and use.

At its simplest this relates to the points about the division of responsibilities made in Chapter 2: work units, exercise sheets, thematic collections, displays, duplicated examples – all these will be prepared by different members of the departmental team to a flexible overall plan, and organized in a central store. The days when each individual was virtually self-sufficient and duplicated his own additional material are surely over.

As I said in the Introduction, my own detailed experience has been in the field of English teaching, and I shall once again illustrate approaches to the organization of printed material in the department by reference to that subject area. I think the points have a wider relevance, and that the problems and procedures are similar to those in Geography, Social Studies, History, Classics (i.e. non-linguistic studies), Religious Education; and that they are met in simpler forms in Mathematics, Languages, and even Music.

The 'traditional' method of organizing an English department's book stock naturally grew out of attitudes to the teaching of the subject (basically, those which presupposed a step-by-step growth into language),[1] but it must also be stressed that in turn the book organization gripped attitudes and teaching approaches so that it was extremely difficult to shift. (Geography and History have had to struggle through similar problems, though Social Studies, generally speaking, developed too late to have to fight this particular battle.) This old approach is well known by all but the youngest of today's teachers: a 'course book' was chosen by the Head of Department. His choice was limited, as to change completely from his predecessor's choice would be very expensive, and such a thorough change was rarely possible in one move. Hence the course-book system had a built-in conservatism compared with the holding of a range of books, which can be changed piecemeal, thus producing a gradual shift year-by-year. The difficulties that this system presents to curricula change, and above all to *personal* teaching, which is closely related to the needs of a particular class, are well known.

---

[1] Cf. *Growth through English, John Dixon*, N.A.T.E., 1967, and reprinted O.U.P., 1970; and my chapter 'Mainstream' in *Directions in the Teaching of English*, edited by Denys Thompson, C.U.P., 1969.

This course book attempted (often with considerable ingenuity and liveliness) to include all the elements presumed to be required for a pupil's 'studies' in English. That some of the elements in the traditional English course book would now be rejected (in particular analytic grammar) is irrelevant to my present concern. *Whatever* the elements, such a book had to be based on the assumption that many thousands of pupils of a given age, but across a wide range of abilities, could base their work on the same single editor's choice of passage, exercises, advice, and stimulus. Such a theory had only the virtues of administrative convenience in its favour: that apart, it flew straight in the face of observable reality. These books were supplemented by 'class readers' (often, indeed, glorying under the title of 'supplementary readers') – novels in class-size sets that were issued, *with little or no choice for the teacher*, on a term-by-term rota: 'Would you like *The History of Mr Polly* or *Thirty-Nine Steps* for 4b this term, Mr Smith?' Thus novels were stretched or chopped, Procrustes-like, to fit the arbitary length of a term. As a last gesture a class was issued, if it was lucky, with a verse anthology, usually for a year! Such a book, though often criticized, but in many ways a miraculous balancing-act of generalized choice, was presumed to contain 'the poems every second-year pupil ought to have met'.

This pattern of annual course books, plus annual verse anthology, plus termly novel will be recognized as the standard pattern that dominated the teaching of English in British schools, and is still to be found in many hundreds of English departments. It presumes standard choice, broadly agreed directions, and is inimical to the personal and the particular. The way it has been transformed in many large English departments is analogous to the shifts in many other subjects as well, and is a typical example of the working out of the advantages of size and variety that I said in the Introduction are there to be exploited in the comprehensive school.

One starts with the assumption that only the broad direction and overall aims are the province of those outside a particular classroom – both external to the school (e.g. editors) and within the school (e.g. Head of Department). Within those broadly agreed aims and selecting from the broadly agreed methods (as formulated by the procedures described in Chapter 3), the individual class teacher is not only the best but probably the only person able to diagnose the particular needs of the individuals in a learning group, and to choose teaching material for them. The object, then, of a Head of Department's administrative procedures should be to allow the class teacher to choose and make available what he judges best for him, this group of pupils, and this particular moment in time. Such a scheme is difficult to administer, but is easier in the large department where purchases can include material of admittedly minority use that could not be justified in a three-form entry school, but which will get well used in a twelve-form entry school. I shall describe the workings of such a scheme as it had developed over many years' experience.

All *sets* of books (whether 'full class' size or 'small' sets) are locked away (one exception is noted later): it is not wise that a large department should have ready access, for confusion and loss will follow. The departmental headquarters contains a *specimen copy* of each book held. These are arranged in types (verse, drama, prose, miscellaneous anthologies) and within these types simply under author. This set of specimen copies (which must not be taken away) acts as a full catalogue, and on the front end-papers of each is pasted a *stock sheet*, which indicates the number held at the last stock check,[1] and which of the two issuing methods apply to that book. The main system is called *Extended Loan*, and a subsidary one *Period Loan*. *Extended Loan* books have one division only – they are split into year 1–3, and 4 and above to recognize the major teaching-group and timetable shift of the school. Within those two age divisions teachers are entirely free to plan the reading for their classes by selecting from the *specimen copies,* and filling in a reservation chit for an approximate date, indicating roughly how long they are likely to want to keep the set. They are encouraged to plan a fair way ahead (though, obviously, the system allows for flexibility and change of emphasis), and can book as many sets as they may think appropriate for a class, relating their time of booking to the momentum of the individual class, and not necessarily the term divisions. These chits are left for the department's librarian (discussed later, on page 65), who sends a note back to indicate whether the books will be available as re-

[1] It is a very bad failure in too many schools to use sets of books that have been allowed by loss or damage to fall below strength: if the method of teaching requires one book per pupil (as is necessary for reading and homework, but not for group or project work) it is a duty of a school to supply each pupil with a copy. Parents can and should complain if this is not possible.

quested. Then on the date requested the set is put out for the teacher with a stock card to sign.[1]

The subsidary system of *Period Loan* is the one in which most, *but not all*, anthologies are placed. These sets are in a series of easily accessible cupboards, with reservation timetables for each set, and signing-out sheets beneath each file. Teachers can send for these as they require them for sporadic use (but cannot issue for homework). This allows a very intensive use of the books, a great range of extracts and poems available to teachers, and the possibility of getting just the right poem for the next lesson unrestricted to a particular editor's choice. The disadvantages of the method are obvious: heavy damage, occasional disappointments when a set proves to have been taken by another teacher, and books not available for homework.

No department, though, is going to find the range of printed books sufficient, and many active departments seem to revolve round a duplicator. It is common sense to formalize these resources so that the efforts of one are made available to the rest of the team. As I write, the Crown Woods English department has some four hundred sheets. To make best use of such resources the following procedures seem wise: (*a*) the stencil for each is filed for reprinting as required later; (*b*) a large number are run off in the first place (say 100); (*c*) these copies are filed in manilla pocket folders with a sample of the sheet pasted on the outside; (*d*) each folder is given a boldly printed serial number and a library pocket and card; (*e*) samples of each are filed in loose-leaf catalogue binders. These are classified as verse, prose, etc., and are cross referenced where appropriate by simply including a second copy of the sample in another reference position. Teachers can then easily find the folder they want, and borrow the pack. Actually I'm inclined to think that such resources should be seen as disposable, with additional copies run off as required.

The last essential point is that breadth of resources must be matched by ready retrieval. In the case of such a collection as I have just described, I think the easiest method is for each person to have a sample sheet of the whole duplicated collection in a series of

[1] Every copy of a book has a departmental stamp, a set number, *and a copy number*. It is a strict requirement that this copy number has to be entered into the teacher's register when the book is issued: this is the only way to limit losses as there is a clear record of which pupil has which particular copy. Schools that do not insist on taking these numbers down suffer ridiculous losses.

personal folders in his teaching room, and that these should be updated twice a year. Certainly a central card index for poetry is required by title, author, and first line with their sources: thus those on duplicated sheets, anthologies in *Extended Loan*, and anthologies in *Period Loan* would come together in the card index.

Such systems will vary from school to school, and are not precisely applicable to all subject departments. However, I am convinced that in the subjects which rely on printed sources one of the most potent decisions that a Head of Department makes is how he organizes his stocks of teaching material, for the method of teaching is strongly influenced by this. And I am further convinced that it is in the direction of variety, flexibility, and availability, with the concomitant requirements of full cataloguing, careful stock checking, and efficient issuing, that each Head of Department must be moving.

Ancillary Assistance
I have already spoken of the certainty that a school needs professional chartered librarians, and a central audio-visual aids assistant. Secondary schools already have ancillary help in Science (laboratory assistants), boys' craft (workshop assistants), and often in the visual arts (studio assistants). One of the clearest certainties of the future is that a study must be made of the needs of the schools for a proper level of clerical and secretarial help.[1] Every Head of Department in a medium or large school should be able as an absolute minimum to have all typing and duplicating done (given adequate warning) by central office facilities. In addition, dictating time (probably by means of dictating machines) will be required for correspondence. It must be stressed, though, that teachers, as a result of their training, outlook, and experience are often poor at using secretarial help to the best advantage. For instance, an office requires a fairly constant work flow: it is impossible to cope with sudden rushes of large quantities of typing and duplicating – yet Heads of Departments frequently create such rushes by hanging on to work and not passing it for typing as soon

[1] Pro-forma are an essential way of rationalizing procedure, saving time, and encouraging a real concern for fundamentals. In a large school a flow of notes is inevitable: the pro-forma is a way of systematizing some of these. A school will need some as a whole (e.g. Record of Interview forms) and a department others (e.g. requests for specimen copies of books, mark sheets, report sheets, and so on).

as possible. Again, the dictating of letters is considerably more efficient in the use of time if a number is done in one session, rather than the week sprinkled with individual letters.

In addition, though, to this urgent need for typing and secretarial help all departments need the equivalent of the Science Laboratory Assistant (perhaps shared between the smaller departments). In the humanities, books, visuals, printed and duplicated sheets, tapes, slides and the like are the raw material, apparatus, and experiments. I take it as axiomatic that the trends in humanities teaching enshrined in a series of Schools Council publications and other now 'standard' points of view *require* ancillary clerical help. The concomitant of flexibility and range of source material is a stock-keeper; and the concomitant of visits out, speakers, and a range of external relationships is a secretary (and adequate phones!).

An Authority and a school can deploy its major resources (not for the moment including teachers) in a variety of ways. These resources include money, buildings, equipment, ancillary staff, printing, and time. The Head of Department will want to ensure that by clarity of thought, breadth of knowledge, efficiency of procedures, and power of persuasion the resources, whatever their limitations, are deployed as effectively as possible. Without this the most enlightened and progressive teaching ideas will flourish but patchily.

8

Student Teachers

How to meet the twin obligations to visiting students and the school's own pupils is one of those many problems that loom so large in the kind of comprehensive school which I am discussing that it has to be considered carefully; it is then found that the very size of the problem makes a solution both easier and more effective. Students from Colleges of Education and University Departments have, of course, always visited schools and spent various lengths of time on 'teaching practice'. However, their distribution was uneven – many grammar schools saw only the occasional student teacher – and it was generally agreed that the effectiveness of the practice period varied enormously. Despite frequently most helpful personal guidance from individual teachers to individual students, it is clear that the 'teaching practice' of many, perhaps most, students in many, if not most, schools has been unsatisfactory.

The whole system of the training of teachers is under review. S.P.E.R.T.T.T. (The Society for the Promotion of Educational Reform Through Teacher Training) was founded in 1968. Typical of the more radical demands is this plea by Eric Robinson, Head of the Faculty of Arts, Enfield College of Technology, to the October 1969 S.P.E.R.T.T.T. conference:

A firm national policy is essential. There is no national policy unless it is to get teachers regardless of what they can teach and how they can teach. If there is a policy on teacher training, let the Secretary of State tell us what it is. . . . Real educational advance is not achieved by merely reforming the institutional machinery of education, but requires reform of the content of education, and this is impossible without radical reform in the way we train our teachers.[1]

There has been a full-scale Government inquiry into the training of teachers: the James Report. Various smaller-scale inquiries have been instituted, such as the Nuffield Project for Research into the Preparing of Teachers for Working with Disadvantaged Children. The National Young Teacher Advisory Committee of the N.U.T. reported the results of an extensive survey in 1969, and summed up: 'There is a great need for change in the training of teachers . . . [we found] serious omissions and inadequacies in college courses',[2] and in a carefully worded inaugural lecture, a recent Professor of Education put the dissatisfaction mildly but accurately when he declared: 'This gulf between trainer and practitioner is common to all professions. But it is wider in the teaching profession than in any other.'[3]

The general dissatisfaction and the gulf reveal themselves with particular force in the experience of school practice. This is a vitally important experience for the student, one which has a future influence for more than the comparatively short period of time would suggest. As Professor William Taylor puts it: 'It seems likely that the time that the student spends in schools during the college course may have a greater influence on attitudes and personal development than any other single aspect of post-school education.'[4] This puts a heavy burden of responsibility on the school, one which is balanced by the fear of what effects the visiting students will have on the pupils. In many schools it is a responsibility that is accepted without real thought, and shrugged off lightly, with a little extra free time gleaned from the periods when the student is left to establish his own uneasy truce in the classroom. This is not the place to discuss fully the possibilities and effective procedures of the practice periods,[5] though one cannot help reiterating that far too little serious thought has been

[1] S.P.E.R.T.T.T., *Newsletter No. 1.*, November 1969.

[2] *The Future of Teacher Education*, N.U.T., 1969, p. 18.

[3] T. H. B. Hollins, *Another Look at Teacher Training*, Leeds University Press, 1969, p. 1.

[4] *Society and the Education of Teachers*, Faber and Faber, 1969, p. 144. This is a most thought-provoking book, and the whole of that section (6) on 'Practical Work in the Education of Teachers' is especially relevant.

[5] For a useful discussion see *Students into Teachers*, Mildred Collins, Routledge and Kegan Paul, 1969.

given to the problems.[1] My present concern is that, if the practice time is to be of the maximum value, it falls to the Head of Department once again to make the broader aims operational. It is he who will accept the student in to the departmental team, and his planning that will make the time valuable. If he accepts the importance, and difficulty, of shaping the practice time for the student, the Head of Department will find the teaching practice not only doesn't harm the work of the classes, but even strengthens the department. It is the basic job of a Head of Department to make it clear by attitude and procedure that the student is, as it were, a fully paid up junior member of the team. And the more fully a student is made to feel a real member of the department, the more he will gain from his time in the school. His contributions to informal discussion and formal departmental meeting are valuable, and if they are valued he will profit more from these sessions.

The starting-point must be the establishing of a close link between the school department and that of a particular training institution. Preferably the school as a whole should limit its student intake to a fairly small number of institutions with practice-session timing of which the school approves:[2] for a school to accept students from a wide variety of institutions with different teaching practice times to bring into some relationship and different authorities with which to establish communications is foolish. Between the school department and its chosen institution (or at the most two or three institutions) there must be a close understanding, so that each knows the other's approaches, appreciates the scope of the work attempted, and is sympathetically aware of the other's strengths and weaknesses. The Head of Department will visit the institution, get to know tutors and lecturers, and grasp the sequence and structure of the course. There will be an interchange of syllabuses, and the College (or Department) will be given lists of books used extensively in the school department for the stocking of the college library. The department's scheme of work will be sent, as well as copies of all school publications, and the more important circulars. Invitations will be sent for all school functions, concerts, plays, and the

[1] Two useful symposiums are *Teachers of Tomorrow*, Ed. Kenyon Calthrop and Graham Owens, Heinemann Educational Books, 1971, and *The Education of Teachers*, ed. Tyrrell Burgess, Penguin, 1971.

[2] Cf. Taylor, op. cit., pp. 161-4 for reference to possible schemes.

like. By all these points, small in themselves, a special relationship is built up, and only within this, I should suggest, can real student care be offered. Such a relationship not only benefits the students; it can be of immense value in the flow of ideas – a two-way flow!

Armed with this knowledge, the training institution will choose its students as far as is possible to fit the characteristics of the particular school. The Head of Department will receive in advance a 'profile' of the student's background, interests, and special skills. A visit will be planned, ahead of the start of the practice period, in which the Head of Department can welcome the new student, describe the department to him, and go over his or her timetable. This is the time when a personal copy of the scheme of work, a few sample books, and any other relevant literature is handed over.

The student's timetable will already have been carefully devised. Each student should largely (perhaps two-thirds of the time) be working with one teacher – best thought of as a 'teacher-tutor' – with whom he will spend sufficient time to get on close terms and whose work he will come to know sufficiently closely for an evaluation of its aims and procedures. However, to work only with one 'teacher-tutor' would be to limit the student's experience and observation. It is disastrous to scatter the work of a student over too wide a range of teachers, for it shatters any continuity and makes a true working partnership with anyone impossible. On the other hand, for a student teacher to work with one teacher only is to limit his or her experience unduly, and to give insufficient points of reference. The ideal seems to be one main teacher for two-thirds of the practice periods in the week, and one-third with some different, preferably contrasting, approaches – perhaps a different type of experience or age. Further, the student's timetable should be planned to give a fair cross-section of classes (by age and ability), but wherever possible it should include all the periods in a week with a class that he joins.

The teacher-tutor's role is one that needs expansion and clarification. Its importance is recognized by only a few training institutions, who pay the school tutors a modest sum for their services. There is no doubt that such financial recognition will become both more widespread and more substantial. Indeed there is a strong case for larger schools having certain teachers given the appropriate status, remuneration, and time to carry out a regular training job. This would help the cause of staff stability by creating additional avenues of promotion in the school, would make the training/teaching worlds less apart, and would help towards better training.

Within the classroom the teacher-tutor will establish a close working partnership. Instead of the more traditional split of: 'observe passively for a while and then take over', he will devise a flexible but progressively more involved sequence. From the start the student will have an active part, however small. He will certainly assist with the advising and checking of individual pupils and their work, and he may well take a part of the class's homework to read. The next period his comments can be added to those of the teacher. At a fairly early stage he should take off a very small group of pupils for a number of periods to do some particular run of work with them. This allows the student to sense the learning processes of such pupils quite separately from having to cope with the complex problems of full-class teaching.

For the early weeks the direction of the work of the class will clearly be in the teacher's hands. However, he will often ask the student to find and suggest particular examples, pieces of teaching material, or processes. The pupils will have the feel that two members of a partnership are working with them. This has interesting and excellent effects,[1] and my experience is that it benefits the pupils enormously. The time will soon come when the student takes substantial sections of the lesson as the dominant partner. Even so, he slots into a framework shaped by the teacher. This means that the student can keep his energy fresh and his ideas sharp for his 'spot' in the lesson, rather than having to dissipate his efforts in, for instance, collecting up homework or settling the class down. The baton is handed from one to another, and the student can polish particular techniques. There *are*, of course, specific techniques, and too often the student is led to feel that successful teaching is a well-packaged mystery that he needs to search for as a whole. What Stravinsky said of the spirit and detail of music is analogous to teaching: 'You do not capture the magic without getting the notes right first.' By the time that the share of

[1] Cf. *Two in a Classroom*, Nancy Martin and others, University of London *Bulletin*. Number 7, Autumn, 1968.

the actual 'teaching' is roughly half-and-half, it is essential that the two members of the partnership are able to evaluate and discuss each other's work. Of course, most of the points will flow one way, but it must be possible for the student to say 'Why did you do that? I should have felt it was too long?' or 'Wouldn't it have been better if . . .'. Certainly students often get insufficient analysis of their lessons; and it is the teacher-tutor's job to do this. Such basic techniques as getting a discussion going, teaching a song, questioning pupils about a statistical table, or introducing a film, need analysis and teaching. Before the class the teacher-tutor never criticizes the student (or should never – it is still a common failing), but afterwards the student deserves a breakdown of the lesson.

The time will come when the the student is determining the direction of the class, sometimes using material suggested by the teacher-tutor but more often found by himself. It is only around this point that the teacher will leave the student for whole lessons. He is not, however, abandoned. He will report back to the teacher-tutor, saying what seemed to go well, and what less well. It is advisable for there to be a fixed weekly meeting between them, when the week's lessons can be reviewed with rather more calm than immediately after each, and detailed problems and successes related to wider and longer-term teaching strategies.

A large department will probably go further than even that. Some central departmental plans will be made to bring the students together, help them share and evaluate their experiences, and relate particular classes to the school as a whole. Either the Head of Department himself, or one of the experienced members of the team with a special interest in teacher training, will have specific oversight of all the students working in that subject area (and others who though specializing elsewhere may have an interest in aspects of the department's work). This 'Student Adviser' (see pp. 19–20 earlier) might well be a teacher whose ultimate ambitions lie in teacher training; he will know in general the pattern of teacher training, and in detail the training institutions from which the students come. He will read the relevant journals, attend suitable conferences, and be familiar with the literature of current ideas in the training of teachers. His first step after establishing the timetable for the students will be to convene a meeting of the teacher-tutors concerned at which the processes described above will be discussed. It is often quite difficult to obtain an understanding and common policy along the lines described earlier and the tradition of 'observer then take over' needs considerable hard work to wear away. He will make sure the teacher-tutors have the necessary information about the students, and will arrange the initial introductions.

During the period of teaching practice he will not only be available for advice and consultation, but he will also have a session perhaps once a fortnight to meet all the students (thus bringing together those from, say, a College of Education and a post-graduate Department of Education). This is a chance to talk frankly and in detail of problems and successes without having the teacher-tutor present. Such sessions could well be capped by formal seminars in those aspects of the subject that the school feels especially well qualified to teach. Such seminars (and more general ones may well be run by the school on broader educational topics) can be joined by any of the teachers who feel they would like to: this bringing together of the young probationer and the student is especially valuable. These should be properly planned sessions after school, in which a particular topic is taken by a member of the school's staff who specializes in this aspect; so that, for instance, the screen, the library, books for backward readers, can be studied. There is a considerable advantage of school-based seminars: not only is the teacher-tutor discussing in the context of his regular experience, but also in a known context of particular pupils, classes, and conditions. This type of seminar stands in that crucial midway position – the position of thought and discussion which I regard as most valuable in all aspects of education, but the one which is so often missed: the relating of particular situations to broader principles by school-based discussion, standing back from, but not away from, the regular daily situations. The teacher-tutor talks about *that* lesson, *this* pupil, *that* piece of writing. The departmental seminar talks about the wider need, broader strategy, lines of approach, next year's classes growing out of *this* year's experience, and links all this to outside knowledge and ideas.

Here as a sample is one term's scheme for students in one department (the teachers' and students' names are fictitious):

CROWN-WOODS SCHOOL: ENGLISH DEPARTMENT

ENGLISH-TEACHING SEMINARS FOR STUDENTS
SPRING TERM 1967

The department's main contribution to student training in English teaching is the close working relationship between the visiting student and the school teacher-tutor. (In addition it is hoped that students will find the general informal day-to-day conversation valuable.) However, the teacher-tutor's first concern is with the joint planning of the lesson sequence, and the sharing and discussion of specific periods. The teacher-tutor, in fact, usually has to take for granted the student's familiarity with the material and 'subject matter' of the full range of English teaching.

The fundamentals of the approach to English-teaching are, obviously, primarily the concern of the institutions giving professional training. However, at such an early stage in the students' practical experience of teaching in the classroom, it has commonly been found that students are not familiar with certain areas of our work, and both students and their college supervisors would welcome more specific and more basic guidance than the school teacher-tutor can give in the normal class-based discussion.

We have therefore planned the following seminars. The scope of these should be clearly understood. In particular, it must be realized that these are NOT planned as a comprehensive course. Indeed the subjects should not be taken as indicating priorities or balance in our concern with the various aspects of English teaching. The topics have been chosen on the basis of experience and our discussion with college tutors to cover some aspects of the work that are essential to the student's time with us and with which it is likely help will be needed.

The approach of each seminar will be practical, posing the questions: What is the relevance of this aspect to the total scope of our pupils' work in English? and: How do we actually set about the work in the classroom? In each case the teacher running the seminar can fairly be described as having some special

experience and additional competence in the area
outlined. Indeed, the teachers named are the
departmental advisers on those subjects.

The achievements of these seminars are
likely to be modest, but we are convinced that
they will be of some real value, if proper
preparation is made. A brief reading list for
each subject is attached, and it will be essential to have read these books in advance. (The
majority are in either the Departmental Library
in room 305, or in the School Library.) It is
presumed that students will be familiar with the
departmental scheme of work.

Seminars will be on Thursday evenings from
4.30 to 5.30 in room 305. Two regular full
departmental meetings are included in the
series, and these are held in room 235 at the
same times.

Students: Miss Penelope (York) and Mr Coren
(Culham) will be here for each meeting, and will
be joined by Mr Star and Miss Richardson (both
from London) after 13th February.

The seminars will be supervised by Miss
Rush, who has organized the programme, and any
problems or queries should be referred to her.

Michael Marland
December 1966

February 2nd: Regular Departmental Meeting.
                 Subject: Accuracy in written
                 work.
February 9th: (Mr Marland) on Newspapers and
                 Advertisements
                 Discrimination and Popular
                 Culture (the chapters on the
                 press and advertising)
                              Ed. D. Thompson
                                       (Pelican)
                 Following the News
                              M. Marland
                                  (Chatto & Windus)
                 Communications R. Williams
                      (Penguin or Chatto & Windus)
                 The Practice of Journalism
                              Ed. Dodge & Viner
                                       (Heinemann)

Looking at Advertising
                M. Marland
                (Chatto & Windus)

February 16th: (Miss Rush) The use of the
                library.
                Please read the relevant part of
                the English Scheme of Work.
                Teaching of English   Chapter on
                                School Library,
                                page 93.
                                Ed. A.M.A.
                                (Cambridge
                                    University Press)
                Teacher Librarian. E. Grimshaw.
                                        (Arnold)
                                Part I   Chap. II
                                    (Book selection)
                                Part II Chap. I
                                (Library
                                        Instruction)

February 23rd: (Mr Wells) Drama in the English
                lesson.
                Experiment in Education - Sybil
                Marshall (C.U.P.) Section 5
                Thieves and Angels - Ed. Holbrook
                (C.U.P.)
                The Bird-catcher in Hell
                Second Shepherd's Play
                Newsom Report par. 477-480

March 2nd: Regular Departmental Meeting.
                Subject: Non-specialist English
                in the Sixth Form
                    (There will be a special
                    collection of sample textbooks
                    available in 305.)

March 19th: (Mrs Lockey) Material for the
                Less Able Pupils.
                Tales Out of School   Geoffrey
                Trease

> Silver Sword Ian Serraillier
> (Puffin or Heinemann)
> Gumble's Yard John Rowe
> Townsend (Puffin or Hutchinson)
> and the poems recommended in
> the syllabus.

March 16th: Mr Harvey on screen (TV and film)
appreciation.
The 'Screen Appreciation' section
of the English Scheme of Work,
and the film sections in:
'Discrimination and Popular
Culture'
        Ed. D. Thompson (Pelican)
'The Popular Arts'
        Hall & Whannell
                (Hutchinson)

March 30th: (Mr Baylis) The Use of the tape-
recorder in the classroom.
Teaching with Tape Graham
Jones (Focal Press)
Broadcasting with Children
Kenneth Method (U.L.P.)

There is no doubt that the scrutinizing of teacher training that I touched on at the start of this chapter will grow in range and intensity in the future, and that fundamental changes are going to be made. It is no exaggeration to say that at a time of major curriculum innovation, a massive extension of the social role of the teacher, and the huge complexity of secondary school reorganization, there is a crisis of confidence in the training of teachers throughout the country. For instance, the Schools Council Working Paper which discussed 'the education of socially disadvantaged children in secondary school'[1] asked:

Does the initial training course adequately prepare its students for the challenges they are certain to meet – not only the very obvious ones in school in educational priority areas, but also those, less discernible, in practically all other schools? Are there

[1] *Cross'd with Adversity*, Schools Council Working Paper 27, Evans/Methuen Educational, 1970.

in-service courses available for those experienced teachers who wish to bring themselves up to date with current developments and new techniques?

It would be surprising if it proved possible to answer such questions with confident affirmatives, since our recognition of the extent and seriousness of the problem is relatively recent, and educational institutions and organizations are often (understandably) slow to react to new demands. All such institutions tend to be conservative – partly, no doubt, because one of their major functions is conservation – and colleges of education are certainly not immune from this general tendency.

The answers that this Working Paper give, and the answers that are beginning to be given elsewhere, involve both a re-structuring of initial training courses and a great emphasis on in-service training and the expansion of the work of Teachers' Centres. What is then needed is in effect a blurring of the distinction between initial and subsequent training: a commitment to teaching is an involvement to an endless process of further training. I have already pointed out (chapt. 3) that the departmental unit is the nation's most significant in-service training medium. The burden of this chapter is that the department's work with students should be a major contribution to their initial training as well as to the necessary blurring of the initial/in-service dichtomy. If the admirable concept of the linked school and training institution[1] is to spread, it is at a departmental level that it is most likely to really flourish. The role of the Head of Department is a crucial one in the training of the nation's teachers.

[1] Cf. 'Children and their Primary Schools' (*The Plowden Report*), H.M.S.O., 1967, paras. 992–8.

9

Parents

The Head of Department's responsibilities towards the parents of the pupils in the school (and, though to a considerably lesser extent, even to the whole of the local community) are usually little appreciated by newcomers, and often barely realized by even well-established holders of such posts. Yet this is one of those crucial areas where the point I made on page 8 is worked out in practice: the traditional role of a *Head* Teacher is changed in its nature, becoming far more active and effective when dispersed and delegated to others in the organization. The Head Teacher of a secondary school is often thought of as its only correct point of contact with the outside world, so that in many schools, for instance, letters about a pupil addressed to 'assistant teachers' have to be passed to the Head for answering. It is he who initiates meetings for parents, and who dominates their form and content. The next decade will surely see a vast expansion in the vigour of the work schools put into building an effective relationship with parents. Equally surely the work must be tackled at a greater variety of levels within the school. The pastoral organization will have a special part to play, but so will the departmental structure, for each Head of Department, especially of the majority-time subjects, must foster interest amongst parents, and answer for the work of their children in his field.

We are now at a special point in considering a school and its parents. We have left the paternalism of the public school tradition ('Boy!' thundered the famous early nineteenth-century Headmaster, James Boyer 'the *school* is your father! Boy! the school is your mother . . . and all the rest of your relations!'[1]), and are growing out of the stony confidence of the grammar school, for many of whom, since 1944 at least, parents have been overlooked because the school had such an elevated privileged position in the educational pecking order. Less easy to cast off is the wretched attitude found in many schools in working-class areas where the schools have for long, and in certain cases with some justice, felt that they were vitually saving their pupils from their parents. At a time when educational ambition is at a higher point than perhaps ever before, the significance of a school's attitude to the parents of its pupils is becoming more clearly realized, and some (but not yet sufficient) evidence is available to help guide a school's steps: this evidence must be assimilated by the Head of Department and used to shape his practice.

When sociology confirms a teacher's observation and experience, it is clearly time to act. The most significant research in educational sociology of recent years, it seems to me, is that which has demonstrated the very close relationship between parental interest and pupil success. It is very clear that all schools, but particularly secondary schools, should make determined efforts to improve the closeness of their relationship with the homes of pupils. At the moment I should say the work of almost all secondary schools in this respect is inept.[2]

There are three reasons for making a special effort:

(i) Parents have a *right* to be 'kept in the picture' as fully and vividly as possible; the educative process is a much richer and more human thing if they can be given an idea of what the teacher is attempting, and why. It is not always realized how anxious many parents are to know more, and especially how desperately inhibited they often feel about making attempts to find out. A *Political and Economic Planning* survey found one in three parents would like more opportunity to discuss their child, and 35 per cent said they did not know enough about the school.[3] When ACE reported on the 'Education Shop' which they opened for a week in Ipswich in 1965, the findings that interested me most were

[1] See the description by Coleridge in *The Christ's Hospital Book*, Hamish Hamilton, 1951, p. 113, and *The Romantics At School*, Maurice Marples, Faber and Faber, 1967, p. 55.

[2] Patrick McGeeney's book *Parents are Welcome*, Longman, 1969, confirms that secondary schools lag behind the Primary Schools.

[3] *Family Needs and Social Services*, P.E.P., 1961, p. 186.

the facts that the shop saw more parents in one week than an average Headmaster in the town *in a year*. Further, and this is the most thought-provoking point, a half of the 'manual' or 'routine non-manual' workers or their wives 'had not set off from home with the intention of asking a question'.[1] In other words, schools have so far hardly started exploring the actual and potential interests; they simply are not meeting a need which is there, though often submerged. Very few teachers seem familiar with the fact that it is the parents of the lower socio-economic classes who feel the most unsatisfied by the information about education currently available.

(ii) In the second place, it is clear how sketchy a picture of the pupils for whom we are responsible most of us have. The classroom and the out-of-school activities (for those relatively few who join in) are patently insufficient to give teachers a well-rounded picture. Teaching is more effective if the school has the necessary knowledge of the pupils, both in a general way (e.g. the feelings of a community towards entertainment) and in detail (e.g. John's father takes him fishing). The Newsom Report pointed out that 'Many situations would be helped simply by schools knowing more of the home circumstances'. Even in specific subject terms there may be gains. F. D. Flowers claims that an understanding of the social background 'may help the teacher to discover suitable content for his English lessons'.[2]

More particularly one can instance cases where specific detail about the pupil is essential in responsive teaching, and this detail is not always gathered simply from seeing the pupils. For instance, I once taught a girl whose writing I could see in a completely different light when her mother explained something the girl would not: any mistakes in a piece of writing done for homework sent her back to the start to re-copy! One might add as a further justification in this direction that teaching can be made more interesting and enjoyable.

(iii) The final group of reasons are the most compelling. Teachers have always known that success in school is not solely related to measurable ability, and a whole series of research projects in the fifties,[3] showed that 'ability' for 'ability' pupils

[1] *The Education Shop*, Lindsay March, the Advisory Centre for Education, 1966, p. 72.
[2] *Language and Education*, Longman, 1966, p. 136.
[3] The Crowther report gave a strong impetus to this line of thinking. H.M.S.O., 1959.

from the lower social classes did less well. One report, for instance, investigating a typical three-stream grammar school found that not only were the initial streamed placings influenced by social class, but later there was a close correlation between movement 'downstream' and the lower social classes – even though as these pupils were heavily concentrated in the lower stream anyway, the overall likelihood of dropping was less than that of the pupils from parents of the higher social classes.[1]

But the sixties produced more sharply discriminated evidence which related progress and failure not just to the broad umbrella of social class, but to the specific element of parental interest. The crucial evidence was the research led by J. W. B. Douglas, for the Medical Research Council, and published in *The Home and the School*:

> The influence of the level of the parents' interest on test performance is greater than that of any of the other three factors – size of family, standard of home, and academic record of the school – which are included in this analysis, and it becomes increasingly important as the children grow older.[2]

Three years later the Plowden report, clearly inspired by these findings, published its own evidence, and the first Statistical Table[3] showed that parental interest is the factor of greatest significance, and that it continues to grow in importance as the pupil leaves the Primary School. The words of the report have central importance for the responsibility I place on the Head of Department in this chapter:

> Our evidence suggests that parents' occupation, material circumstances and education explain only about a quarter of the variations in attitude, leaving three-quarters or more not accounted for. *This implies that attitudes could be affected in other ways, and altered by persuasion* ... Our findings can give hope to the school, to interested parents, and to those responsible for educational policy. Parental attitudes appear as a separate influence because they are not monopolized by any one class. Many manual workers and their wives already encourage and

---

[1] See *Down Stream, Failure in the Grammar School*, Dale and Griffith, Routledge and Kegan Paul, 1965, p. 15.

[2] J. W. B. Douglas, *The Home and the School*, MacGibbon and Kee, 1964, p. 57.

[3] *Children and their Primary Schools*, H.M.S.O., 1967 p. 33.

support their children's efforts to learn. *If there are many now, there can be even more later.* Schools can exercise their influence not only directly upon children but also indirectly through their relationships with parents.[1]

And in a book that grew out of the Plowden research,[2] Michael Young and Patrick McGeeney describe how as outsiders they were able to *increase* parental interest and thus pupil success by modifying the activities and procedures of a school.

We know, then, that existing parental interest is unmet, that mutual knowledge of parent and school is valuable, that parental interest is not tied to particular social classes; it is a key factor in pupil progress, and, above all, it can be attracted and fostered. Schools consistently overrate their success in this field,[3] and we have very clear evidence of the gap between teachers' aims and parents' expectations in the Schools Council's survey *Young School Leavers, Enquiry 1*.[4] What should the Head of Department do? It is convenient to look at his responsibilities to parents in three ways; (*a*) the need to report on the individual progress of pupils; (*b*) the need to explain various stages in the school, approaches to the subject (e.g. policy towards examinations), specific decisions and reasons for the grouping and placing of pupils; (*c*) the need to meet, engage, and develop general interest in the subject and in schooling. Thus (*a*) concerns the individual pupil; (*b*) the school organization in which he or she is working; and (*c*) the philosophy and method of the subject. Looked at in one way there are three broadening stages, but it will also be seen that they are circular, because the third feeds the first: it is a limited departmental policy that stops at the first (*a*), and fails to appreciate that the parents' interest in their own pupils is sustained and made more effective if it is given a context and direction by (*c*).

The basis of the department's success in reporting on individual progress is the atmosphere of individual concern which the Head of Department must always reinforce, and to which the school reporting system and record system both contribute. He will

---

[1] Ibid, paras. 100 and 101; my italics.
[2] *Learning Begins at Home*, Routledge and Kegan Paul, 1968.
[3] e.g. In one Junior School the Head Teacher said that between 80 per cent and 90 per cent of parents called in to see him during the course of the year. Evidence drawn from questioning the parents of all the children on the roll revealed a total of only 50 per cent. See also *Enquiry 1*, H.M.S.O., 1968, Part II, Chapter 6.
[4] H.M.S.O., 1968, especially Chapter 2, Part II, Chapter 1.

interpret the school's formal reporting-to-parents system to his department so that these are as full and specific as possible. Comments on reports should be precise, encouraging, isolating aspects of the subject where particular effort is required, and frank. This is not the place to survey reporting systems in general,[1] but it is necessary to stress that good reporting cannot be left to chance and normal professional skill – too often the comments will have the opposite characteristics to those qualities I mentioned. Two of the commonest faults are vagueness ('She must make a greater effort') and euphemism – which misleads parents not used to reading between the lines ('He seems to be under the apprehension that he can succeed without effort' or 'He is apparently devoid of all seriousness').

The formal report, though, must be supported by individual 'interim reports' or letters whenever there is a need. The tradition that only a catastrophe leads to communication is a bad one. A note of approval, a note expressing worry about a certain aspect of a pupil's work, especially a rapid indication to parents if there has been a failure of one sort or another (e.g. over a homework assignment) are necessary moves by the subject teacher or department head whenever possible. And, one ought to be able to say 'of course', the Head of Department must be willing to see personally any parents who feel the need to talk some matter over, however slight.

But, as I suggested earlier, the informed interest of parents in the progress of their children depends also on an understanding of the school and the subject. A Head of Department must seize every opportunity, and devise fresh ones, to put this kind of information across. His battery of approaches will include whatever school publications there are (and there is a strong case for a regular periodical for parents), circular letters to certain sectors of the parents on particular aspects (e.g. the value of a field trip, or the need for pupils to have mathematical instruments), the opportunity to speak at general parents' meetings, displays (e.g. samples of books read in English classes), posters, and special meetings, as I shall describe later. In these days of curricula innovation,

[1] Lesley Keating's book. *The School Report*, Kenneth Mason, 1969, is the only full-length study, but though it has some sound points it is not very deep. A. W. Rowe's article in *Where?*, Number 17, 1964, is brief but interesting. I have contributed a study to the symposium on pastoral care in this series.

and in schools with a necessary (and usually desirable) complexity of organization, it is the more necessary – and the more difficult – to give this information. When it is attempted, there is a temptation to overplay the experimental details, giving parents an over-stressed impression that their children are virtually guinea-pigs. They may often need persuading that some shift of teaching approval is worth while. The Schools Council *Working Paper* on *Social Services and the Curriculum*[1] describes a difficult example: it is a definite but difficult departmental duty to put across to parents the aims and values of the work in hand.

It is also important to avoid the educational jargon and textbook style in writing to parents. Without being falsely jaunty or imitating the more ridiculous journalese, it is possible to develop a relaxed informative style.

It is not, though, merely a matter of explaining the changes and stages in the school: the Head of Department needs to actively *encourage* interest. One of the most effective means of doing this is by a variety of kinds of meetings: not just passive listening to talk, but active ones as well; meetings in which parents can sample teaching materials, take part in actual work, and get the feel of the activity. For instance, handling equipment in a mathematics laboratory, or using percussion instruments in a creative music lesson are tangible ways of introducing new approaches, and often interest hitherto unconcerned parents.[2] I have had considerable experience with a variety of explanatory evenings for parents which have convinced me of the value in illuminating, interesting, and giving confidence. The success recipe is difficult to establish. For instance, on one occasion I attempted to combine the opportunity for parents to speak to individual teachers about their sons or daughters – and this considerably overloaded the evening. The best mixture has appeared to include some brief explanatory talk, or demonstration lesson with pupils, and a demonstration lesson with parents. Such evenings, I have found, work better if they are narrowed in scope, and take some especial aspect of a subject, one perhaps through which parents can help their children.

[1] 'It will require considerable diplomacy on the teacher's part after the event to meet the criticism that "I send my child to be educated, and not to help Mrs Smith."' Working Paper No. 17, H.M.S.O., 1968, p. 2.
[2] For a number of specific schemes, which though largely drawn from Primary Schools nevertheless are helpful comparisons, see *Parents are Welcome*, Patrick MacGeeney, Longman, 1968.

an invitation

9th October, 1967

Dear Parent,

Parents, I know, are always anxious to encourage and help their children with their school work, and particularly with their homework. In the first and second years of a new school it is quite common for parents to feel some doubt about what is in fact the most valuable help that can be given. As you will have read in the Bulletin, we are arranging an informal evening that may go some way to help answer this question:

"Your English homework is..............."
October 18th at 7.45 p.m. in the Library

On this occasion we shall try to be as realistic and practical as possible and to give plenty of opportunities for parents to ask questions. The evening will start with a short demonstration lesson given to a first year class, which will lead to the setting of homework. In this way you will see a typical pre-homework lesson. I should like to follow this with a demonstration lesson with a number of parents whom I hope will volunteer. At the end of this we shall distribute duplicated copies of a few example of pupils' work resulting from a similar lesson. After a break for refreshments we shall be able to compare parents' reactions to the pupils' homework with our reactions. The whole evening will last a little under two hours, and I hope will be of great interest.

Accommodation will be very limited, as I am anxious that everybody shall be able to hear and see clearly. If you would like to come I should be grateful if you could return the slip at the foot of this letter to your son's or daughter's English teacher by Friday, 13th October, stating clearly whether your request is for one or two seats.

Yours sincerely

Head of the English Department

To the English teacher of _____

Class _____

I should like one/two tickets for the Parents' Meeting on October

Signed _____

Date _____

The title of one such evening explains its purpose: '*Your English Homework is . . .*' It was almost certainly the most successful explanatory evening for parents that I have been responsible for, and the success came from earlier mistakes. This time the scope was not too wide, and the sequence of events was very carefully scheduled. The letter opposite went home to all the parents of pupils in the first year.

The audience were seated in three banks of chairs facing inwards. The centre space of the horseshoe was taken by tables for a class, and a group of first-year pupils were waiting there. The Head of Department explained to the parents something of the reasons for homework, what kind of work is set, how it arises. Another teacher then gave an actual, though curtailed, lesson to the class of pupils. The lesson grew out of a poem, and each member of the audience had a copy. Mainly a lesson of question and answer, opinion and anecdote; there were a few inaudible remarks, but such a lesson is in fact very absorbing, even entertaining, and holds the audience much as a play might. The lesson led towards the setting of an actual homework assignment on the board, and copied down by the pupils. Thus the parents could see precisely what kind of thing led up to the baldly noted assignment that their sons or daughters might have brought home. Of course, such a lesson is a strain to take, for it can in no way be rehearsed, and works best if it is as normal as possible, for the pupils simply one in its natural sequence. It does have a faint air of artificiality certainly, but my repeated experience is that after a few moments the flow of the lesson itself absorbs the pupils and they forgot the audience.

This was followed by a similar lesson, using different material, given to a volunteer class of parents themselves. More artificial still, but curiously effective in communicating what a real lesson feels like. After a break for refreshment, photocopied examples of pupils' work were distributed for discussion and questions. The same work was then handed out *as marked* by the teacher. The evening ended, as it must, by a free flow of questions and challenges, in which the Head of Department calls on whoever is the most suitable of the team to answer a particular point.

There are clearly a number of variations possible for such an evening. It will be found to both interest and inform parents, and is an important way by which the Head of Department can convey his team's approaches to parents, and thus enlist their informed support.

If recent trends in secondary education are to have their full impact, I think we must accept Dr Michael Young's remark that: 'Teachers will have to be taught almost as much about ways of educating parents as they are now about teaching children.' We need firstly to broaden our view to take in the reactions and influences of parents. At the same time we need to gather specific ideas for putting this belief into effective practice. Perhaps this note may serve as a contribution towards this movement. I am sure that if it is to succeed, it requires the ingenuity and effort of Heads of Departments.

10

The School

Most of the considerations raised in this book have looked inwards, as it were, to the subject teachers responsible to the Head of Department, and to the pupils considered as members of the classes which the department teaches. But the Head of Department has other responsibilities and must have other perspectives as well. Often subject enthusiasm narrows his vision. This chapter is a brief note on his role in relationship to the school as a whole. Looked at in this way the Head of Department's position can be seen to be pivotal: interpreting the school to the members of the department, and putting to the school (through the meetings of Heads of Departments, and by individual meetings with the Headmaster, etc.) the attitudes and findings of the department.

The implications of the first of these I have already discussed in Chapters 3 and 4. The second has in practice two sides to it: the Head of Department can be seen as a delegate charged with expediting a department's needs by doing his best to gain facilities, permission, time, staffing, and agreement to the many adjustments to routine required by the department's activities. He can also be seen as an adviser to the school, whose central policies will be affected by the corporate view of the Heads of Departments. Looked at from the first point of view his views are legitimately sectional: he is rightly struggling for the needs required for the pupils' success in his subject area; looked at from the second point of view the Head of Department is not acquiring for his department, but is using his intimate knowledge of a team of teachers and a subject area as evidence for his advice on broader educational points. Headmasters who talk about their 'Cabinet' may be suspect for grand delusions, but there is a real sense in which a Head of Department's position (unlike a Head of School or Head of House) is analogous to that of a Cabinet Minister. He is both after what he can get for his specialism and anxious to advise and influence broad central decisions as well. We could call these two roles of influence: the requesting and the advising.[1] The second is the more major, but the first, it is worth remembering, is felt the most frequently and with the most immediate concrete effect. Tactically it is worth getting the first right if the second is to be influential. Views on attitudes to discipline or the structure of the sixth form are going to be heard with less sympathy after, for instance, a series of visits which has cut into the time of other departments without proper warning.

A: *The Requesting*

From the discussions and delegation described in Chapters 2 and 3 will have come a clearly articulated subject point of view; this will have to be quantified in terms of staffing, amount of time, disposition of time, accommodation, finances, and equipment (as discussed in Chapter 7). As a preliminary to putting specific requests to the Headmaster (or to whomever he has delegated these responsibilities) it is well worth finding out as much as possible about the academic structure of the school and its timetable mechanics. It is then necessary to ascertain the appropriate times in the year at which decisions are made: the year has a necessary pattern of decision making, and it is unreasonable to present points too late in the sequence. In general it is true that the majority of departmental requests, however intricate, can be met if they are clearly put and presented at the appropriate time and as part of a continuing dialogue. It is too common for departments to feel aggrieved at the disposition of the timetable, without having ever troubled to propose alternatives. Normally it is wise to sum up such ideas in a carefully set out memorandum that tabulates the needs economically. These basic annual considerations are becoming more complex year by year as the tyranny of a weekly-based timetable is progressively loosened. Further, variety

[1] Very little study has been made of the roles within a school, but readers will find helpful thinking in *The Sociology of the School*, M. D. Shippam, Longman, 1968, and a more general study of teachers' roles in *Society and The Teacher's Role*, Musgrove and Taylor, Routledge and Kegan Paul 1969. See also the other volumes in this series.

of pupil grouping, and range of option possibilities are additional factors. In this situation the Head of Department needs to be alert and ingenious if he is to succeed in making adequate provision for the subject for which he is responsible.

Apart from the major negotiating for a suitable place in the annual disposition of resources, there are the frequent requests for special arrangements: changes of teaching room, pupils to be released from lessons in other subjects, and so on. The larger and more complex a school, the harder it is for the originator of a scheme to foresee all its implications for other sections of the school. It is therefore essential to plan early and bring proposals clearly before anyone likely to be concerned. A department planning a visit, for instance, would be well advised to circularize names of the proposed pupils or post a notice weeks in advance: if there are no objections the details can be confirmed a week ahead of the event. When complicated adjustments to routine have to be arranged, for a visiting theatre group to perform in the school hall for instance, an effective method of tying the details together is to stencil all the details on one circular, clearly divided up under headings which indicate who has accepted which responsibility. Not only is it usually quicker to do one memorandum for the whole event than to do a note for each teacher concerned, but also such a circular allows each person affected to see how his action fits into the scheme and relates to what others will do.

The general point, then, is that an enthusiastic concern for the needs of a department must be tempered by an understanding of the needs of other sections of the school, and a grasp of ways of requesting, informing, and organizing so that the one ploy does not upset the rest of the school.

B: *The Advising*

The Head of Department, as we have seen, is one of the key advisers to the central policy-makers of a school (whatever their nomenclature). He should have two special qualifications. For one thing he should know his team of teachers so well, and should have engineered informed discussion with them so fully, that he can speak *for* a number of staff, confident that he will be regarded as their spokesman. If staff feel unconsulted, their legitimate complaint in a large school is only indirectly to the Head Teacher: the vast burden of consultation must be undertaken by the various team leaders in the organization. A Head Teacher can't reasonably be expected to consult in detail, with, say, a hundred staff. The Heads of Departments are expected to have close consultation with their teams.

Secondly, a Head of Department speaks out of his knowledge of a particular subject, frankly from the point of view of a scientist or an English teacher. This is something which the sensible Head Teacher will cherish, for each specialism has its own viewpoint which is admittedly partial, but also has insights to some extent denied to others. There are likely to be ways of looking at such school questions as 'discipline', relationship with parents, the sixth-form curriculum, to give only a few examples, which relate to the particular viewpoints of the subjects. I do not wish to exaggerate this: mathematician and historian may well agree. What I want to stress is that the teachers' insight into pupils and the effect of school policy on their lives varies according to the kind of activities with which they engage the pupils' minds, emotions, and interests. There is a real sense, for instance, in which a craft teacher, working almost entirely with smallish groups of pupils in largish rooms, and in practical situations in which most of the time pupils are working at their own pace, just does not understand the problems and aims of much else that happens in the week. At the same time, though, such teaching situations reveal aspects of pupils which are totally hidden from others.

So armed with both these kinds of knowledge – his team's discussed and formulated views, and his subject's pupil insights – the Head of Department should not only be prepared to join central discussion, but also to survey the general direction of the school and initiate inquiry and discussion where he sees the need. He doesn't wait to be asked. This means, of course, that a Head of Department should be well read and as widely knowledgeable as possible about events elsewhere. Schools are not the isolated communities that they were even ten years ago, but there is still an urgent need for deliberate effort to acquire information: how does another school allocate time in the third year? Are there schools that combine this or that subject in the first year? What forms can the morning assembly take? . . . and so on. The advice of a Head of Department must be more broadly based than the single school.

There is ample evidence from fairly recently reorganized comprehensive schools in many parts of the country that the large (or even rather small!) comprehensive school can have considerable confusion, dissatisfaction, and feeling of apartness among the teachers. Whatever method of full staff conferences and so on that is devised, it will fall to the Heads of Departments by way of this pivotal function to ensure that the school understands the department's thinking, and that the department feels a part of the large community and not a splinter group.

Out-of-School Activities: a note

One of the most pleasing features of British schools has for long been the vigour and variety of the voluntary out-of-school activities. Based on the personal interests of individual teachers, a range of clubs and activities have brought teacher and taught together as partners in a shared enthusiasm. The voluntary and individual basis of such activities puts the Head Teacher of a school in a paradoxical position: should this be an area of school life that is left strictly alone to discover its own momentum and direction, or does it need help?

Once again, the Head of Department has a vital role to play: a vigorous voluntary extra-curricula life does not just happen; it can be seeded and fostered. The danger of looking at this departmentally, is obvious: not all activities (e.g. chess or orienteering) have an obvious link with a school subject. Also too close a copying of the departmental structure will kill any of those valuable enthusiasms on the part of teachers of other 'subjects'. Yet, these dangers having been admitted, it seems to me to remain a clear departmental duty to survey on the one hand the range of activities which might grow out of the subject area, considered in its broadest sense, and on the other hand the known, even if only half articulated, interests of the individual teacher. After all it is the Head of Department, not the Headmaster, who is likely to know these best.

There seem to me to be four principles for a healthy out-of-school life: (a) opportunities should be planned so that as far as possible all kinds of pupils have a chance to participate. This, for instance, casts some doubt on the notion of 'the school play' or 'the school magazine', because if drama or publications are organized in that way only a few are involved; (b) the extra-curricula should grow out of the curricula, and in its turn feed back into and enrich the day-to-day classroom work. There should be wherever possible a continuum between classroom activity, voluntary informal after-school clubs, and more formal public presentation where relevant; (*c*) if the activity is to flourish and have continuity, it will need nursing by a senior member of staff – usually the Head of Department – to ensure that the individual teacher has recognition (*most* important) and encouragement, and to plan for continuity when he leaves. Schools are littered with the discarded debris of old enthusiasms waiting to be picked up by someone not yet appointed. It is possible to prevent this with proper planning.

As an example of a suitable range, perhaps I could briefly sketch the activities growing out of English at Crown Woods School, each of which has had continuously vigorous activity without interruption for a span of years.

(i) Paperback bookstall, open twice a week and carrying a large and varied stock with a high turnover, and considerable pupil interest. The stall depends on the close and knowledgeable involvement of a teacher *who knows the stock*.[1]

(ii) Drama: after-school clubs for each year group, and four or five public productions a year, planned to cover the age range and offer a conspectus of types of drama and types of appeal, from a sophisticated eighteenth-century literary anthology to *Billy Liar*. One year's programme, for instance, included a modern play about teenage difficulties, *Johnny Salter*;[2] *Zigger Zagger*[3] by Peter Terson, *Mother Courage* by Bertolt Brecht,[4] an informal programme of items by younger classes called *Drama Workshop*, and *The Crucible*,[5] performed by the Sixth Form – all in all a fair conspectus of dramatic interest. There are also a very large number of theatre visits.

(iii) Film: both film-making group, and a Film Society, showing to third years and above those interesting and worth while recent films that they would otherwise not have seen.

(iv) Broadcasting: the conversion of an old chair store into a

[1] For further practical details see the article on this subject by Marilyn Davies in *The Practice of English Teacher*, Ed. Graham Owens and Michael Marland, Blackie, 1970.
[2] By Aidan Chambers, Heinemann, 1968.
[3] Penguin, 1970.
[4] Methuen Modern Plays, translated by Eric Bentley, 1962.
[5] Heinemann, Hereford Plays, 1967.

recording studio has led to both a club activity and special projects working on documentary, dramatic, and pure sound (often for drama and film effects).

(v) Recommendations: a small point this, but related to the previous four points, a display board of cuttings, advance notices, and posters is maintained for recommended films, plays, radio and television programmes.

(vi) Publishing: an occasional (three or four times a term) duplicated literary and polemical magazine is produced.

(vii) 'Personal Choice': twice a year the English teachers invite 'personally' a number of senior pupils to a mixture of cider, food, and readings in the library. These readings are invited in advance, but unstructured, and the resulting mixture from pupils, visitors, and teachers is a most enjoyable evening.

Such a range of activities, I should suggest, makes a genuine contribution to the life of the school. It is one that depends on the personal willingness and excitement of teachers, but it also requires the planning, balancing, and encouraging of a Head of Department.

11

Conclusion

The success of a comprehensive school depends to a very great degree on the understanding of their jobs by the Heads of Departments. As an increasing number of such comprehensive schools are created, a greater variety of patterns of responsibility are developing, and in many schools the simple traditional subject groupings are being dropped, and in their place new amalgamations (Art and Craft, Craft and Science, etc.) are being devised. I seriously doubt whether all these amalgams will prove successful. The essential points of my description, however, strike me as applicable to any such pattern.

There is no doubt that the evolution of comprehensive schools is a painful process – largely because it is rarely possible to stand back from the work of the moment to plan the work of the future. The process is rather like trying to rebuild a factory without stopping the assembly line. One of the greatest difficulties is that there are usually no 'job specifications' for the key posts, and too many people in too many schools have been obliged, or have chosen, merely to improvise in the new situation. Although the precise patterns of delegation will vary from school to school, the health of any comprehensive school depends on these key roles being defined and understood. Without that, size becomes pointless, and variety becomes an amorphous mess. The departmental structure is one of the focusing devices of such a school, but it must not become a self-contained empire. Paradoxically it is through a well-developed departmental structure that meaningful freedom comes. There are too many large schools where each teacher is fighting his own battles, having local and isolated successes, but only despite the system (or lack of system). In such schools the new Head of Department wonders where to start, for he has no 'Department', only a title and a Burnham allowance. (It is very rare, incidentally, for a proper 'hand-over' to be accomplished, and the number of Heads of Departments who are given an outline document detailing the department and its routine obligations is minute.) It is a very difficult task to lead in such a situation, but his first job must always be to weld the team of teachers together.

The personal qualities required for such a post are certainly daunting: experience of teaching at a variety of levels of ability; wide knowledge of the subject area, and of other aspects of education; the knack of relating well to people, and being able to serve their needs and their special qualities; immense energy; a highly developed sense of organization. Perhaps among the most important is the ability to articulate points of view clearly and persuasively. (Larger schools are demanding a greater facility with words, both spoken and written, than their smaller predecessors.) None of us has all these qualities, we surely feel, in sufficient strength, but I hope the summing up in this book will help newcomers to use their skills to the best advantage.

No one will come to the points in this book completely new, but my experience suggests that much of it may be new to many, and the points which I have found most need stressing relate to the concepts of the advisory team – that is the delegating of ideas and thinking. Paradoxically the Head of Department who delegates and shares out in the kind of ways I have suggested in Chapter 2 finds his 'power', far from being eroded, is increased and given more force by such an arrangement. (In the same way, a Head Teacher who uses his senior staff in this way will find his true position strengthened.)

Leading a department in a large comprehensive school is, one must admit, very exhausting. The total number of hours involved and the total quantity of energy used are very high indeed. It is few but the complacent who often feel on top of the situation – and it is a strong criticism of the educational system that this should be so. In essence the Head of Department's personal problems are those of establishing a tolerable hold on priorities. The sheer pressure of decisions required and initiatives to take will surprise the teacher who moves from a tripartite school system, and often, indeed, the new appointment who has had previous experience in a less senior post in a comprehensive school. There is an absolute need for rigorous and energetic handling of all paperwork. The priorities are difficult to establish and there is a continuous tension in the Head of Department's task – arguably more tension than in the post of Head Teacher itself.

The tension comes from the problem of balance: balance between the overall school requirements and the narrower subject needs; between organizational possibilities and theoretical ideas; between flexibility and rigidity; between teacher and teacher; between pupils and teachers; between encouragement and direction; criticism and praise. Above all, the sharpest problem of balance is between long-term planning and today's problems.

I think that such a job is one of the most stimulating in the whole of education. I hope that I have made it clear that the Head of Department is not the Senior Geography Master writ large. He is the catalyst and co-ordinator of a team of people; he is the link between that team and other groups; his aims are to create atmosphere, encourage thought, and devise procedures. He must continuously pick up and give back, so that there is a mutually stimulating, and mutually supporting team.

A Head of Department's Reading List

The number of books being written on educational topics (though not always the topics one should wish for) continues to increase, whilst it really does seem that the number read by teachers remains stubbornly low. As well as books in his subject area, the whole of the educational list would, I suppose, be relevant to the aspiring Head of Department – for he should be knowledgeable and widely read as well as experienced. This list has a modest task. It is a possible answer to the question from an applicant for a major Head of Department post, 'Well, what should I have read?' The list is deliberately fairly short, but each title is, I have found, stimulating and directly relevant in its different way. The first two sections especially are, obviously, no more than representative.

In footnotes to the text, full bibliographical references have already been given to all the sources for quotations and facts. In addition, a number of suggestions for further reading have been made where a particular book or article has seemed very closely connected to the point being made. Some of the titles are naturally repeated here. Fuller bibliographies are included in a number of the books, and those in Rubinstein and Simon's *The Evolution of the Comprehensive School*, and my own *Pastoral Care* might be looked at first.

Background Thinking

There is a substantial library of studies on the broad social, economic, political, and human problems of modern education. This is a small selection of books which, although not concerned specifically with comprehensive schools, explore some of the fundamental problems that have to be considered in working in such a school.

Bernstein, Basil, 'A Socio-linguistic Approach to Social Learning', in *Penguin Survey of the Social Sciences*, Penguin Books, 1965

Craft, Raynor, and Cohen, eds., *Linking Home and School*, Longman, 1966

Dale, R. R., and Griffiths, S., *Down Stream – failure in the Grammar School*, Routledge & Kegan Paul, 1965

Douglas, J. W. B., *The Home and the School*, Routledge & Kegan Paul, 1964

Floud, J. E., Halsey, A. H., and Martin, F. M., *Social Classes and Educational Opportunity*, Heinemann, 1956

Hargreaves, David H., *Social Relations in a Secondary School*, Routledge & Kegan Paul, 1967. An interesting sociological study with implications on grouping and organization. It brilliantly reveals how a sub-culture is built up in the school

Jackson, B., and Marsden, D., *Education and the Working Class*, Routledge & Kegan Paul, 1962

Marland, Michael, *Pastoral Care*, Heinemann Educational Books, 1974. A substantial study of the various ways of organizing care and guidance, including a detailed analysis of roles and functions and patterns of responsibility

McGeeney, Patrick, *Parents are Welcome*, Longman, 1969

Mays, John Barron, *The School in its Social Setting*, Longman, 1967

Aspects of the Curriculum

Barnes, Douglas, et alia, *Language, The Learner, and the School*, Penguin Books, 1971. A consideration of the place of language in learning in all 'subjects'

Beswick, Norman W., 'Instructional Materials Centres', article in *The School Librarian*, Volume 15, Number 2, July 1967

Britton, James, *Language and Learning*, Penguin Books/Pelican, 1972, paper

Gunn, S. E., 'Teaching Groups in Secondary Schools', a good introductory survey in *Trends*, No. 19, July 1970

Half Our Future, the Newsom Report, H.M.S.O., 1963; Although there is relatively little attention to school organization, the survey of attitudes and subject teaching is still a mine of ideas

Hooper, Richard, ed., *The Curriculum*: context, design and development. Oliver and Boyd, 1971. A very good Open University anthology

Kaye, B., and Rogers, I., *Group Work in Secondary Schools*, O.U.P., 1968

Marland, Michael, *Towards the New Fifth*, Longman, 1969. A discussion on the part to be played by English and the Humanities with older pupils after the raising of the school leaving age, with some possible schemes for linking subjects

Schools Council, *Community Service and the Curriculum*, being *Working Paper No. 17*, H.M.S.O., 1968

'*Cross with adversity*': *the education of socially disadvantaged children in secondary school*, being *Working Paper No. 27*, Evans/Methuen Educational, 1970. A lengthy discussion, though unfortunately marred by vagueness and lack of clarity and restricted by an apparent middle-class bias. The chapter on the training of teachers is by far the best, and has implications for all aspects of department leadership

The Certificate of Secondary Education: The Place of the Personal Topic–History, being *Examination Bulletin No. 18*, H.M.S.O., 1968

Society and the Young School Leaver, being *Working Paper No. 11*, H.M.S.O., 1967

Whitfield, R. C., ed. *Disciplines of the Curriculum*, McGraw-Hill, 1971

Worral, P., et alia, *Teaching from Strength, an Introduction to Team Teaching*, Hamish Hamilton, 1970. A practical and lively account, with well worked out details

Comprehensive Schools

Benn, Caroline, and Simon, Brian, *Half Way There*, McGraw-Hill, 1970. A painstaking survey, which patiently and with understanding compares most aspects of the existing school. An invaluable book

Burgess, Tyrell, *Inside Comprehensive Schools*, H.M.S.O., 1970. Although written for the layman, some chapters are among the best accounts of the reasoning behind such schools

Halsall, Elizabeth, ed., *Becoming Comprehensive*, Pergamon, 1970. A series of case histories written by the Head teachers of a number of schools

Halsall, Elizabeth, *The Comprehensive School*, Pergamon, 1973. This is a detailed survey of the available research. Very practical

Holmes, Maurice, *The Comprehensive School in Action*, Longman, 1967. A fairly routine account of a typical comprehensive school structure

I.A.A.M, *Teaching in the Comprehensive School, A Second Report*, C.U.P., 1967

Miles, Margaret, *Comprehensive Schooling*, Longman, 1968. The Headmistress of Mayfield School, London, describes her approaches in a readable account

I.L.E.A., *London Comprehensive Schools, 1966*, Inner London Education Authority, 1967. Obviously such a survey dates rapidly, but the data on school organization and the work of departments is worth study

Miller, T. W. G., *Values in the Comprehensive School*, Oliver & Boyd, 1961. A classic study which endeavours to plot the overall aims of the schools

Monks, T. G., *Comprehensive Education in Action*, N.F.E.R., 1970. A statistical research survey with an excellent section on pastoral care

Monks, T. G., *Comprehensive Education in England and Wales*. The first of the N.F.E.R. surveys, this examines structure, organization, use of teachers, etc

Pedley, Robin, *The Comprehensive School*, Penguin, revised edition 1969. The best general theory and survey

Ross, J. M., Bunton, W. J., Evison, P., Robertson, T. S., *A Critical Appraisal of Comprehensive Education*, N.F.E.R., 1972. The most important of the N.F.E.R. studies, covering most aspects of the school work

Rubinstein, David, and Simon, Brian, *The Evolution of the Comprehensive School*, Routledge & Kegan Paul, 1969. Such a historical survey, which charts clearly the steps to comprehensive schools via 'multilateral' ones, may seem academic. In fact this book is essential reading if the problems and possibilities of today's schools are to be fully understood by the teacher

Miscellaneous

Cave, Ronald, *All Their Future*, Penguin, 1968

Clegg, Alec, and Megson, Barbara, *Children in Distress*, Penguin, 1968

Cox, C. B., and Dyson, A. E. (eds.), *Fight for Education: A Black Paper*, Critical Quarterly Society, 1969. This, and the successors, *Black Paper Two*, and *Black Paper Three* are collections of essays attacking 'progressive' trends. Many of the criticisms are weakly or inaccurately written, but some of the criticisms are pointed and worth considering

Rubinstein, David, and Stoneman, Colin (eds.), *Education for Democracy*, Penguin, 1970. An uneven collection of essays claiming to be a 'radical manifesto on British education'. A number of contributors have important points about comprehensive schools and their underlying thoughts

Schools Council, *Young School Leavers*, being *Enquiry* 1, H.M.S.O., 1968

Taylor, William, *Heading for Change: the management of innovation in the large secondary school*. A workbook for teachers and students. Routledge & Kegan Paul, 1969, rev. ed., 1973. This collection of simulated material covers the whole range of comprehensive school problems in a recognizably realistic way. This book originated in a Harlech Television series for teachers, and is concerned not so much with new ideas, but how they impinge on a school

Young, Michael, *The Rise of the Meritocracy*, Thames & Hudson, 1958, and Penguin Books, 1961. A brilliant satire that postulates the ultimate situation if selection were to be extended and refined

Periodicals

Comprehensive Education, the journal of the Comprehensive Schools Committee

Forum, a thrice-yearly journal 'for the discussion of new trends in education', published from 71 Clarendon Park Road, Leicester. Has specialized in the comprehensive school, and ways of working with mixed-ability groups

Trends in Education, H.M.S.O., quarterly. Despite the occasional article which seems remote and unreal, this is a good combination of theoretical consideration, comparative survey, and practical suggestion edited by the D.E.S. 'Subject' articles are written to interest teachers in other disciplines, but the best contributions tend to be on aspects of school policy